Unconditional Love

Unconditional Love

My father killed my mother...this is the true story
of how I learned to forgive him

NATALIA AGGIANO

WITH VANESSA HOWARD

JOHN BLAKE

Published by John Blake Publishing Ltd,
3 Bramber Court, 2 Bramber Road,
London W14 9PB, England

www.johnblakepublishing.co.uk   facebook
www.facebook.com/Johnblakepub   twitter

twitter.com/johnblakepub

First published in paperback in 2008
This edition published in 2013

ISBN: 978-1-78219-360-9

British Library Cataloguing-in-Publication Data:

A catalogue record for this book is available from the British Library.

Design by www.envydesign.co.uk

Printed in Great Britain by CPI Group (UK) Ltd

1 3 5 7 9 10 8 6 4 2

Papers used by Publishing are natural, recyclable products made from wood
grown in sustainable forests. The manufacturing processes conform to the
environmental regulations of the country of origin.

Every attempt has been made to contact the relevant copyright-holders,
but some were unobtainable. We would be grateful if the
appropriate people could contact us.

DEDICATION

NATALIA

This book is dedicated to my dear mother – who always showed me unconditional love. Never was there a love as great as that of our mother. My brother, you are my world, my everything, you make me so proud to be your sister, our bond will never die; my sister – my love for you is stronger than you will ever know; my eldest brother – for the path we each have to walk. To the Todd family and the Picot family – friends are God's way of apologising to us for our families.

And finally, to my father – who taught me about forgiveness and unconditional love.

VANESSA

First and always, for DJH, and my family – I'm truly blessed. And to the Cafe Valance girls, for their tireless wit and wisdom.

ACKNOWLEDGEMENTS

Vanessa would like to thank the following for their help and support: Daiana Allen, Daniel Aggiano, Pete Broughton, Sue Hunt, Wensley Clarkson, Clive Hebard, Professor Kevin Browne, Reverend Peter Corcoran, Geoff Howard, Vivienne Howard, Jo Picot and Helen Todd, and staff at the North Linconshire reference Library.

SPECIAL THANKS

First to Vanessa Howard. I couldn't have done this book without you. You are an amazing lady and have helped more then you know. Your patience and kindness has been amazing; my mum would be so proud of you. Thank you for helping me with this book, you have done an amazing job and I hope you are as proud of it as I am.

To my dear mother Elva Aggiano. Without your love in my life I wouldn't be who I am today. I miss you so much and I now know that you are at peace. I know you will be proud of this book. Please watch over me and the family.

To my father. I miss our chats so much; I miss surprising you with a visit as well as our walks together. Thank you for making me a better person and for finally allowing me to have a real father–daughter bond.

To Daniel Aggiano. What can I say? You were the best thing to happen to me when I was younger. I remember you being in Mum's tummy and how when you were born, I would watch over you as you slept. Even though you are 10 years younger then me, you have always been my rock, you have always been at the end of the phone, always greeted me with your special hugs. Thank you, I can never truly thank you for being the amazing brother you are. I will always be proud of you. I love you millions, nice one brother!

To my sister. Thank you for all your help with the book, I love you more then you know! Here's to trying to get to know each other again and becoming sisters. For too long we have been too distant. I will always be there for you.

To Helen Todd and family. You have been a friend since school, you have been there through the good and the bad. I couldn't ask for more in a friend. You're an amazing person with so much love to give. Believe in yourself! Thank you for being such a good friend, thank you for all the times you let me stay over for free and for putting up with me. Let's hope soon the wedding will be set so I can be a bridesmaid.

To Joann Picot and family. You have been more then a friend to me, you have been my saviour, the number of times you put a roof over my head and fed me. Your shoulders have always been there to lean on. You're an amazing person. I am proud to call you my friend. Thank you so much for being in my life.

To Karen Kelly. You have been like a mother to me and I love you like a daughter. Thank you for always being there for me and for always making sure my hair looks fab. You are such an amazing woman and I am proud to be able to say you are in my life!

To all my friends: Anna Wallace, Gavin Potter, Mark Fillingham, Russell Ahearne, Janice Stallwood, Claire Bray, Sharon Warwick, Carl Tilly (aka Scumbag), Mike White, Steven Green, Dad – Tony Wingate, Eleanor Whitby, Tracey Camelo and Toby Dodwell. You are all special to me in your own way. There's not enough space to say what you all mean to me.

To Joey Downes. I am so glad you came into my life. You make me smile and giggle, you have opened my heart again and given me so much. You're amazing, be strong and be proud of who you are.

To Francesca Zanellotti. So glad I met you. I know we will be friends forever.

To my work team: Granddad – Bob Weir, Dad – Rob Green, Uncle – Malcolm Howell, Brother – Steve Claxton, Manny Bisran – Brother and 'work husband' Paulo Lopez. You make me smile and laugh every day. I have never met funnier people than you lot, you're the best work team ever.

To Fionnuala Carrabyne. No matter how long we go without speaking, you are always there for me. You are such a special person to me. I love you with all my heart and I hope married life is all you ever wanted. May all your dreams come true.

To Craig Taylor. I am so glad I found you as you are such a great guy. Make sure you look after her or you're in trouble!

To John Sample, Rachel Hart, Lee Keith James – the Teeside Massive. Thank you for making me feel so welcome.

To Penny Coomes and Anna Cappellini. Thank you for

always making sure Daniel has someone to catch him when he falls. It means so much to me to know he has you in his life.

To Melissa Eiler. You have helped me so much with my mum's website and you have been a great support. I know our folks are together watching us. Your kind words and support have been amazing and it's great to know you feel the same loss as me.

To Karen Gibbons and Theresa Walsh. You have both been through so many bad things in life yet survived. You have bettered your life and shown the world what you can do. I am so proud of you and all the strength you have.

CONTENTS

THIS IS YOUR FINAL WARNING

My dad knew he had a few calls to make. He would have to telephone the receptionist at the plastics factory where he was working to let them know that he wouldn't make his shift that afternoon. He had already called the police, telling them he had killed his wife and that they should come quickly as he didn't want anyone else to find her that way.

By 'anyone else', he meant his sons, my brothers. The youngest, 9-year-old Daniel, was playing outside with friends; the eldest, Emmanuele, was on his way back home with fish and chips for four. Another call went to my sister Daiana. He told her what he had done and asked her to come home to 'take care of your brothers'. He was sure that she would obey him.

When the police arrived, they found the door to our family home open and my dad in the hallway on the phone, motioning them to follow him into our front room. Two officers followed him and found my mother's bloodstained body. She was lying on her back, her head facing towards the kitchen, which Mum would have known was the nearest exit out of the house. One of the officers radioed back to Scunthorpe police station saying: 'It is as per the phone call.' This was necessary, as in the minds of the other officers called to the house, they imagine it would turn out to be a hoax.

A policeman checked Mum's neck to try and find a pulse but it was clear that she was dead. He then noticed the axe lying to her left-hand side, as well as her chest wounds, and guessed they were the result of a knife attack. The policeman was struck by how calm and cooperative my dad was as he stood over her.

He had been calm since Mum had stopped struggling at some point during his attack, during the twelve times he had stabbed her with our kitchen knives and hit her with an axe. Her attempt to escape him had failed. She had not listened to his 'final warning' to return to him and, as she fell face forwards onto our living room rug, my father's victory was complete, she would never leave him again.

This was our house. It was somewhere Mum knew so well, somewhere she had been so proud of, a home to her as wife and mother. For now, her children were elsewhere and we were all that mattered to Mum. She had given up so much to raise us and had sacrificed so much trying to make her marriage work. All she had strived for was now in tatters; her home now little more than a murder scene and she herself was the victim. Now she lay on a rug she had chosen, staring lifeless at the ceiling as her home filled with police officers.

After she lost her fight for life, Dad had hugged and rocked my mum, stroking her face and talking to her in Italian. This was my dad at his most loving – he called it 'caressing'. It was how he would hold her from time to time on our sofa, telling her she was beautiful and that he loved her. My mother never truly believed him and would push his hand away. Now she was his completely. He stood calmly as the police turned to him and he told them: 'I have killed her body to save her soul.'

The police prevented my brothers from entering the house. Daniel was playing in a street across from the back garden. He had heard the sirens but thought little of it: Old Crosby isn't a rough part of Scunthorpe but it's urban enough for sirens not to register as unusual. My brother Emmanuele had done as he was told, as he always did, and was making his way home with the carefully packed fish and chips when the police approached him. I don't think my father would have cared if Emmanuele had managed to get in and confront him. Dad was at peace with what he had done; his tears came later.

I was back in Cleethorpes, wondering where Daniel and Mum were. Within an hour, there would be a knock at the door and my life would be torn apart. And what made matters so much worse was that when the two police officers stood in my doorway, I knew why they were there. Since the moment I'd woken up that morning, I had tried to find Mum. She wasn't in her flat so I called my dad's house. No answer, so I called my sister. No answer on her mobile but when I rang her work number, I was told that she was away from her desk. I called my mum's mobile. No reply. That's when I knew. It didn't make sense that no one was around to pick up a phone.

When the police spoke to me, I said, 'He's killed her, hasn't he?' What they couldn't know was that my cold fury was directed as much at my beautiful mother as it was towards my father, the killer. Only the evening before, my mum had sat beside me and said that she was going to see Bruno, my dad. I was incredulous; I couldn't believe it as it had taken her years of courage to finally leave him. Why, only a few weeks later, would she want to see him? I was sitting in the bath, getting ready for a night out, we were chatting as we often did now that we lived in the same apartment block.

With Mum living upstairs, I'd often call her in and we'd chat, even if I was taking a bath. Since leaving Dad, we'd spent hours talking and I loved it; it was so different from the mum I knew when I was growing up. For once, she wasn't cooking, cleaning or walking around with that look of worry and concern, wondering what would be the next 'transgression', the trigger point for my dad to lose his temper. In my small bathroom, it was purely mother and daughter time and I'd always try and make her laugh as I talked to her about whatever was on my mind. She had the most amazing green eyes and all I wanted was to see them light up when I talked to her.

Those few weeks had been better than I could ever have imagined. In fact, it had been the best six weeks of my life. It felt as if the nightmare was finally over. For years, I had begged and shouted at her to leave him; I'd told her I wished he was dead. At last, she had left him. She called me and asked me to help her move while Dad was at work and we'd done it. Within a few hours we packed up her life and moved her out. And Mum had begun a new life, living in a flat only two floors above me, and it really did seem as if the violence and abuse had come to an end. For me, the icing on the cake was that Daniel was with us too. My little brother, the one thing that had kept me smiling as I grew up living under Dad's controlling anger and rage.

Now Mum was telling me that she wanted to pick up her mail, that she felt that my dad should be allowed to see Daniel, and also that Daniel missed his friends and it would be a chance for him to see them. As she talked, I could tell that something far darker was going on. There was a shadow in her eyes even as she smiled and tried to sound matter of fact. In truth, I was a little scared. What was going on? I asked her outright. She said, 'Natalia, I think if your father sees me again, he will kill me.'

Despite being immersed in the hot water of my bathtub, I went cold. I was accustomed to Dad's violence. For years I had suffered at his hands and I felt I knew every nuance of his fury and his demand that we obey him, as we would the word of God. Yet I felt that what Mum said was impossible. I asked her again what was happiness and then I made it clear that she shouldn't go. What she said has stayed with me and it always will: 'Natalia, I love your dad. I am not in love with him, but I love him for who he is, not what he does. Just like you. You are my daughter and you have done wrong in your life, but I love you for you, not what you do.'

She was adamant that she would go back to the man it took nearly thirty years to leave, I begged her to take me with her and she agreed. She promised that she'd call for me. Instead, the only knock on the door came from the police. My beautiful mother was dead. My first feeling wasn't one of anger for the horror inflicted by my dad; it was anger towards my mum. Why she would put her life into his hands once again? Why, if she had the slightest doubt, would she visit him and allow herself to be left alone with him? I felt that if you fear for your safety, if you have the slightest concern that you will be in danger, you make sure you run from it, not towards it. And Mum didn't merely have doubt. She *knew*, and she let him take her from us. My life ended that day, 24 May 1997. In the desperate years that followed, years when I tried to find the answers to my mother's actions, my dad's evil and the devastation left in its wake, I have slowly had to rebuild my life.

It has taken ten painful years. In that time, there has been so much self-destructive behaviour, things I regret and grief I still harbour. It's a time that took me back to my father, to years of visits to the high-security mental hospital where he was imprisoned, through his agonising death – ten years during which what was left of my family reached breaking point, when I was spat at in the streets for caring for my father, when I uncovered a terrible secret I never sought and I have since had to learn to bear. I have learnt what it means to truly love, to love without anger – an unconditional love that sustained my mother and a love that, ultimately, is the gift she left her children.

CHAPTER ONE

A SEASIDE CHILD

My mum was born in Cleethorpes, a seaside town in Lincolnshire, on 24 February 1950. She was christened Elva and was the second and last of two children born to Harry and Lily Winfarrah. My mother's sister, Jean, was born some ten years earlier, which seems quite a gap and I'm not sure whether or not it was planned.

Elva is an unusual name. My grandmother once told me it meant baby eel but I later found out that a baby eel is an elver, so I still wonder where she came across it. As a child, I liked the sound that it made but I never found out why my grandfather, a stern man, would have allowed my grandmother to choose it for his daughter. As a Christian name it must have been unique in Cleethorpes, but I can imagine my grandmother sticking to her guns once she'd decided that it was a name she liked. Although always very respectable, in some ways my grandmother was unusual for her time. She was independently minded, read a great deal and even travelled abroad on her own. Her own mother had run a village shop; Lily also had a good head for business and soon established her own shop selling household products.

My mum spent most of her childhood just outside Cleethorpes, in a village called Thornton Curtis, where my grandmother ran her shop. One of only three, it was an important part of the community. My grandfather was a labourer. Looking back, I can't imagine how my grandparents came to be together; my grandfather was a big man but the general opinion was that he was more brawn than brains. From time to time, you could sense my grandmother's frustration with him and I don't believe they ever truly loved each other. Years later, I found out that she had been in love with someone else but that he had chosen to marry another woman, and so, broken-hearted, my grandmother accepted the next offer of marriage that came along.

My grandmother was quite well educated and bookish and seemed to look down on her husband and his unskilled working life. If she had concerns early on in their marriage, by the time I came along things had settled into sort of stalemate between them. They led their lives separately even though they continued to live under the same roof. I suppose today they would simply have split up, but back then it wasn't the done thing. They were probably just one of many couples who learned to live their own lives in parallel, going through the motions of family life, with friends probably in much the same situation. Harry had his workmates; he could drink in pubs where the 'lounge' was separate from the bar and where women were expected to sit, if they came out at all. It was expected that men and women had little in common except the responsibility of family, and so I'm not sure either of them grieved too much for the way they played out their lives.

Their house was modest and was always kept neat and tidy by my grandmother. I liked her. After my grandfather died, and towards the end of Mum's life, Elva and her mother seemed much closer. While I can't remember much about my grandfather other than his sheer size, I still have a clear picture in my mind of my grandmother. In fact, she looked like everyone's grandma, with her short, permed grey hair and unfussy cardigans and comfortable shoes. She had a gentle smile and liked to sit for photos with us. I think she was proud to be a grandmother. She and Mum would meet for coffee and chat about people I never knew, and they were probably the most relaxed they ever were in each other's company. It wasn't the same with my grandfather. All I can remember was that when he was around, my mum and grandma would be quieter and I didn't like to look at him for too long. He never seemed happy in the company of women and certainly wasn't comfortable with children. Distance suited him best.

When we were little, we would sometimes visit Cleethorpes and although I was too young to realise, by then it was a town way past its heyday. In the nineteenth century, the railway was extended to the town and it became hugely popular. Donkey rides, a 1,200-ft pier, a concert hall and busy promenade meant the resort was packed with holidaymakers throughout the summer. But by the time my mother was born, the pier had been breeched and the seaward end demolished, reducing the pier to just over 300 ft. The concert hall had burned down and post-war austerity meant that everything looked a little tired and shabby. But throughout her life, Mum loved the sea and was always glad to spend time walking along the seafront.

My grandmother was 40 when Mum was born, which was probably pretty unusual then. Had they decided to try for one more child or was she 'caught on the change'? It was never spoken about. The age gap didn't help my mum's relationship with her sister, Jean. Perhaps Jean felt Elva was my grandmother's favourite daughter, but whatever the root cause, they were never close. The person my mum cared most about, or was happiest to talk about, was her best friend Diana. She lived nearby and despite being three years younger, they were close and Mum had very fond memories of their friendship. Despite marriage, children and moving away from each other, they stayed in contact until the end.

Mum's early years were far from ideal, however. At school in those days, you could be hit for not paying attention or find a hard blackboard rubber flying your way if you were caught talking. Home life was strict, too. My grandfather was not affectionate and despite her early efforts to be accepted and loved by her father, I think Mum was aware of his disapproval. Although she was growing up in the 1950s, my grandparents were brought up in another era where the most important thing was being seen to be 'respectable' and 'proper'. That came first, no matter what. What they truly thought and felt was mostly left unsaid. There would be a ritual of tutting and eye-rolling as my grandmother traded gossip about people and stories of bad behaviour. She was sure the world had taken a turn for the worse.

In her eyes, it must have. By late middle age, she had moved into a time when what mattered most wasn't respectability but being true to your feelings. That could mean ending an unhappy marriage, coming out as gay, having children by different fathers or simply not caring what your neighbour thinks about you. My grandmother saw this as the breakdown of decency. It wasn't just the attitude of youngsters either: in the 1960s, the Government was making changes she could never approve of, such as legalising abortion and decriminalising same-sex relationships. Anything positive that might come hand in hand with the changes, such as not having to live a lie, was beyond her.

My grandparents were never openly loving or communicative, so Elva grew up in a household where she learnt to second-guess what her parents expected of her. I don't think it was easy for her. Her happiest memories weren't of spending time with her parents but of playing with her dog, a border collie cross she took everywhere with her. As she grew older, life at home became difficult as she clashed with her father more and more. She was very different in character to him: she was full of life and her temperament somehow suited her red hair. It wasn't auburn but a vivid red, something she hated at the time, but by her late teens it had darkened and became the kind of thick and straight hair that women today pay a fortune to try and imitate.

By the time I was growing up, Mum had put on a lot of weight and felt very self-conscious; she hated mirrors and photographs. Dad had told us all how shy Mum was, and how much he had taken this quiet girl under his wing. I grew up unaware that this was far from true and that as a young woman, she was vivacious, rebellious and surrounded by friends, all looking to enjoy life to the full. The picture Dad painted, and which Mum gave lip-service too, was so very different but it would be years before I discovered why they both felt it important to give this false impression of her early life.

What I did know was that Mum went to primary school at Thornton Curtis and then to Baysgarth Secondary Modern in Cleethorpes. This was back in the days of the 11+, when you could be pretty much written off from the address you gave and the way you spoke. I don't think anyone had high hopes for academic success for my mum; she suffered from a mild form of epilepsy and was not even put forward to sit her 11+. For those who passed, this was a passport to the local grammar school, where you would be prepared for a job with prospects, teaching or in an office. If you failed the exam, this meant spending what was left of your time in school at a secondary modern, where the girls would learn to bake a Victoria sponge, sew buttons and keep a grocery budget. There was no support for anyone with a condition like Elva's and so she was told not to expect to stay on at school. Girls from secondary moderns were expected to follow a path from schooling until 15 or 16 to a local job in a shop or café and then marriage. Once children arrived, they became full-time mums or might have a part-time job for 'pin money'. At least by the mid-60s, there were plenty of jobs available and young people could get out and start to earn a wage, part of which they'd give their parents to help towards running a household, but the rest was theirs to spend.

But it wasn't a bad time to be alive. Unlike the post-war and austere 1950s, with its rationing and 'make-do-and-mend' culture, there had been a real shift. There was far more stuff to buy in the shops, and there was good music to listen to and buy, music my grandfather hated, that was loved by teenagers. Clothes, hair and make-up changed too. Young women no longer dressed like their mothers and my mum was confident enough to wear mini skirts, even though she risked her dad's fury. By this point, Elva was regularly clashing with her father; he was strict and controlling so she spent more and more time away from the house. Despite this generational clash, there was a sense that life was getting better and you could expect more from life than your parents ever had. They had grown up learning the hard lessons of life with war and the Depression, and so naturally they must have felt that their children lacked respect and were too eager to suit themselves and chase good times.

On leaving school, my mum got a job in a biscuit factory in Grimsby and later, in a bakery in Scunthorpe. She was just 16 and was enjoying the fact that she was earning money alongside other girls intent on having fun as well as working from nine till five. Inevitably, that meant meeting men, blue-collar and office workers who would come into the bakery at lunchtime and chat to the girls. It must have been good fun: a bit of banter that makes the working day fly by for everyone.

My dad's background was very different from Mum's. Since the early 1950s, Italians had started to arrive in Scunthorpe and elsewhere in the north of England looking for work in the steel industry. It made economic sense for them, and no doubt they accepted that they had to trade the blue skies and warm weather they were used to for a wage in bleak British industrial towns because their weekly pay packet could support whole families back home. When I hear people complain now about economic migrants, I think of my dad's generation and how willing they were to give up everything they knew to work hard and secure a future for their families. It's a very human instinct and I'm sure if Dad was a young man now, he'd still do the same thing.

My dad's eldest brother had already worked in the area for a few years and he found a way for my dad – Bruno – to join him in 1966, working for British Steel. My father's family were from Brindisi, a harbour town on the south-east coast of Italy. It's an ancient town that has been burned to the ground any number of times as it was fought over repeatedly, but it was always re-built because it had such an important natural harbour. The British even built links there once the Suez Canal was open but by the end of the World War II, the city was suffering from low employment and increasing levels of poverty. It was common for young men to leave Brindisi behind as they sought work elsewhere and almost certainly some never planned to return.

I don't know what my dad thought when he left his home town. Perhaps he saw it as no more than an opportunity to make money. Whatever he thought, he would have had no idea that he was setting sail for the place where he would murder the one person he said he truly loved, and where he would ultimately see out the last of his days in prison. My dad was the fourth of nine children – two had died in infancy – and they were all packed into a modest apartment in the town and pretty much lived from hand to mouth. Bruno's life was made all the harder when his father died when he was only 12. At that point, his schooling ended and he adopted the role of head of the household. He was forced to work to support the rest of the family, initially finding any menial jobs available around the harbour.

His family were very traditional and women were expected to stay home, raise children, cook, clean, and above all, obey their husbands. This was how my dad grew up. He saw little of his father as work took him away from the family home, even as far as America for a few years. Despite my Italian grandfather's ambition, the family couldn't rely on him to send money to them on a regular basis – first, because he was not always in work, and second, because, if rumour were to be believed, he had more than one 'family' to support. Nothing was ever openly said about this but much later my mum told me that my dad's father had a reputation as a womaniser and a heavy drinker.

Not that my Italian grandmother could do anything about this, whether the rumours were true or not. No matter how badly her husband might behave, Italian wives were expected to put up with their lot, even if that meant huge fights at home. Divorce was simply unthinkable; this was Southern Italy, and very backward it was too when it came to ideas of social change. In Brindisi, life was expected to go on as it had for generations, the church was a big factor in everyone's life, and beyond the cathedral in the centre of the town, there were at least another fifteen or so churches serving a small population. But the rituals attached to the Church were as important as its religious teachings, giving a daily framework, sense, rhythm and comfort, no matter what the day-to-day existence might throw at families, beyond the christenings, weddings and funerals.

Although my dad grew up in a traditional household, his brothers and sisters were not as devoutly religious as he was. Dad came to view his priest as a second father and while his brothers went out drinking, he preferred to spend time helping the priest run the local youth club. Dad embraced religious teachings wholeheartedly. He could have turned away from religion – as I later did as an act of rebellion – but for him, it was the basis of his entire understanding not just of how the world was, but also how it should be. He had the Church, his mother and his siblings, but I can only imagine what an example he was set by his own father. Now I wonder if there were echoes of it in the way he ran his own family – the expectation that as the 'man of the house', he would always be obeyed no matter how unreasonable his behaviour might be. And perhaps his views were backed up by what he was taught in church. 'Let wives be in subjugation to their husbands as to the Lord, because a husband is head of his wife as Christ also is the head of the congregation… The wife should have deep respect for her husband.' (Ephesians 5:22, 23, 33).

How a man should act if he felt that respect was not forthcoming was another matter, but all that was to unfold later. Back in 1967, there was a sense of optimism and excitement; for my parents there was the promise of decent wages and they had their whole lives ahead of them. The way Mum and Dad told me the story of how they met could not have been more romantic, I always thought. When I was little I asked Mum to tell me the story time and time again – I was told that at work one day, the other girls behind the counter begged Mum to join them at the community centre, where there was to be a body-building competition that evening. Mum was 17, and apparently she was not really one to go out that often. She was unsure but her friends kept on at her all day until she finally agreed to meet them.

That evening, despite having second thoughts, she set off to see her friends. And who should be taking part in the competition but Bruno Benito Aggiano. My dad wasn't tall, but he was handsome: typically Italian with olive skin, dark hair and brown eyes. But the first thing that struck anyone who met him was how physically fit he was. He was a weightlifter and a cycling fanatic; throughout his life, if he ever had an opportunity to cycle, he would do so for mile after mile. He took a lot of pride in the way he looked and because of this, he made an impact whenever he walked into a room.

I was told that Mum could hardly bring herself to glance at him. She told me that she never dreamt in a million years that he would look her way, she felt her friends were so much prettier, slimmer and never as tongue-tied as she was and so she could barely believe it when Bruno walked over and began to talk to her. That was the story I grew up with, and I liked to hear how my quiet mother was swept off her feet by a handsome stranger. Dad's English would have been heavily accented – it remained so throughout his life – yet he could read and write fluently in English, and he was effortlessly confident too. But I wouldn't say this was arrogance, more a steely assurance. He could also be a great storyteller and people were always drawn to listen to him; his whole manner must have impressed my mother. To find a man, an older man, giving her quite so much attention must have turned her head. And my dad was much older, by almost ten years. It's only now as I approach 30 that I realise just what that means.

As a girl, I just listened to my dad and took it at face value when he said: 'Natalia, seek out older men – women need to find themselves an older man.' But the difference between a 17-year-old girl and a 26-year-old man is vast. I can't help thinking that it was a lifetime of experience, so no wonder Mum was blown away. This good-looking man was making her his focus and it's no surprise that this was a life-changing experience for her.

As my mum told it, their meeting was fate. If she hadn't turned up that evening; if she hadn't listened to her friends, and if she'd decided to stay in her room, unsure of what to wear, then yes, her life would have been very different. What path would she have taken? Would she have found happiness with another man, and another family and be alive today? Or was there something else in her life, her short life, that left her vulnerable and led her to a man who would torment her?

It would take many years before more pieces of the puzzle were given to me. And now, when I look back at the picture postcards of 1960s Cleethorpes, it's no longer with the same innocent eyes. Part of my mother's life was destroyed in that fading seaside town… And it was an explosive and dark secret that led her silently into my father's destructive hands.

CHAPTER TWO

AN ITALIAN BRIDE

It must have been a whirlwind romance. At least that's what I've always imagined and what I was told. Mum was swept off her feet, and Dad was ready to marry her and take her off to enjoy a very different and perfect new life.

My dad was sure he wanted children and he wanted to provide for them in a way that his father had not provided for him. He wanted to move back to Italy with his new bride, to enjoy life in the countryside, to have a simpler and healthier way of life in the sunshine, far away from the rain-filled skies of Humberside. What my grandparents on my mother's side thought about this I was only told in part, much later. There's little doubt that my grandfather was unhappy. Bruno was Italian, a Catholic and an older man: no matter how little interest he might have taken in my mum's upbringing, he would not have been happy to be the talking point of the village, the man whose daughter was

13

with 'an Italian'. He put his foot down, saying he thought the match was a bad idea and that Elva was too young to be thinking about marriage. Yet marry they did.

Many years later, after my mother's death, I sat down and did the maths. Mum was just 18, and pregnant, when they married in July 1968: my sister Daiana was born six months afterwards. What was all the more remarkable was that they married in Brindisi; to be married there, in a Catholic church with a priest, would have been exactly what Dad wanted. The fact that Mum was pregnant must have forced my grandfather's consent. It was an all-too common fact of life back in the 1960s. For girls who found they 'had to get married', a quick wedding was the best way to remedy the gossip and give an air of respectability back to the family.

What my grandmother thought, I don't know. She can't have been thrilled but she did believe that once your bed was made, you had to lay in it – after all, that was what she herself had done. If Mum was foolish enough to allow herself to become pregnant then she would have to live with the consequences. No matter what lay ahead, Elva would now have to find a way to cope and support her new family. I have tried to imagine what she must have felt as she set sail for Brindisi. She was leaving everything she'd ever known – her family and friends, particularly her best friend Diana; her whole way of life. When she and my father married, she also had to renounce her faith and become a Catholic. At that stage, the Church wasn't a big part of her life, but all the same, this meant a definite break with everything she'd ever known.

I have seen a picture of Mum taking communion and it threw me at first as I couldn't understand what was being placed on her tongue. It was a communion wafer, there to represent the body of Jesus Christ; to remind us all what debt we owe Jesus Christ who gave his life so that we might save our immortal souls. This symbol of blood sacrifice, set in an ornate church, would have been an experience very far removed from Mum's few visits to church when she was growing up. She would have known how to sing 'All Things Bright and Beautiful', how to say the Lord's Prayer and not fidget through well-meaning sermons. But now she had been thrust into a world with a new set of litanies, where she was expected to repent her sins in the confessional and accept that the path to God was through the priest. She listened to Latin, some of the words haunting and beautiful such as 'Ave Maria'. If anything might have reminded Mum that she had left her old life behind, it would have been time spent in the ancient church and the faith of her husband and his family. Perhaps, most of all, she would have found herself experiencing so much that was new in a town where no one spoke English. Dad had taught her a few words, greetings really, in Italian, but the scale of the changes that lay ahead of her couldn't possibly have dawned on her until she took her first communion kneeling next to Dad. She would soon be a new mother in a foreign land, entirely alone and dependent on her husband and his family.

Yet somehow she must have felt that she was doing the right thing. Dad was fully confident that it was for the best. There had been some moments of unease back in Cleethropes. Dad had tried to impress on Mum how much he loved her and how easily upset he was to see other men talking to her. He said that no one would love her as he did, and so it wasn't surprising that other men's attentions would make him unhappy. If she had any sensitivity and wanted to make him happy, she should realise that. Mum tried to explain that it meant nothing, that it was often just boys she had known since she was in school, but soon she found it was easier to simply avoid getting into conversations with men than to risk hurting her new husband's feelings.

Dad also pointed out that she needn't spend so much time with Diana. She was no longer a child, she was a woman now, and she should look to the future and their life together; it was time to stop having schoolfriends. Dad could be very intense; he wore his heart on his sleeve and he steadily chipped away at Mum's willingness to fight back. If she cared for him, he cautioned, she should back down rather than risk upsetting him and find herself in an argument that could cause lasting damage to their marriage. He would resolutely run through his logic time and time again. I've met very few people since who can convince or sway someone's opinion as well as Bruno could, and over time, Elva found herself slowly giving in. She may have felt then, as many women did, that it was right for men to be possessive and demand their way. In those days, men were expected to know their own minds and to be the stronger one in the relationship; it was all part of the bargain of being cared for.

There was no doubt too that Dad was homesick and Mum felt for him, of course. He missed the weather and the ease of life back in Italy. He painted a picture of how good life could be and how much easier it would be for them to rent a family home with land to spare there. When news came that there were new opportunities to work near Brindisi, Dad was sure it made sense to return home. He'd be back in the arms of his family, with a job and plans for a life for his new family. Mum was persuaded and began her goodbyes to family and friends. In truth, she welcomed a new start to her life as well; a chance to leave Cleethorpes behind. She wanted to escape and life as Mrs Aggiano seemed to offer her what she craved.

But it was still a huge step to take. Mum never spoke about her first thoughts and feelings when she arrived in the harbour town of Brinisi, but the experience must have been overwhelming for her. She had never travelled far and even though she had grown up next to the sea, she found the landscape was very different; this was the Adriatic, not the North Sea. Southern Italy is warm, dry, and at first sight, beautiful. The architecture is nothing like that of Humberside: Brindisi is dominated by the harbour and the medieval cathedral at its centre; around the square are other ancient buildings and monuments, and a seminary that stores old artefacts including a marble vase said to be the one that Jesus used in his first miracle when water was turned into wine at a wedding in Cana.

But Brindisi is also home to apartment blocks and buildings built after the war, and it was in such an apartment block that Bruno's family lived. This probably wasn't how Elva imagined she'd find the Aggianos, cooped up in close proximity, all within shouting distance of their mother, Nonna. Meeting Nonna must have shattered Mum's tentative hopes of finding acceptance. Any bride wants to be welcomed by her new family and a language barrier would make anyone hope for signs of a warm reception all the more – a hug perhaps, or at the very least plenty of smiles and encouragement. Mum must have been mortified by the way Nonna received her.

It was only when I was a teenager that she let me know just how unwelcome she was made to feel. This went way beyond the natural anxiety of Elva being a foreign bride; Nonna's hostility was open and no matter how Mum tried to appease her over the years, nothing was good enough. Nonna despised the 18-year-old foreign girl. She hated the fact that she was English and that she wasn't a true Catholic; she would never, ever be good enough for her son. Mum's hopes of being welcomed into the arms of her new family were completely crushed, and what added to her humiliation was Dad's complete refusal to challenge his mother. What unfolded must have terrified Mum. Far from tackling his mother's prejudices, Mum had to watch as Nonna wielded her cold fury to try and control not only what Dad said and thought, but the actions of her other children too. Nonna was determined her children would always defer to her: her sons may have married and started families of their own but their first loyalty was still to their mother. She felt it perfectly natural to try and pass judgement or dictate how things were run in their households, and no one seemed willing to stand up to her.

It's hard to imagine the power this tiny woman could command. She was skilled in using anger and guilt to coerce her children into falling into line, long used to commanding her large family, and far from being happy to see them leave the nest, her need to be involved in their lives only seemed to grow. With her hair in a severe bun and always dressed in black, she had a vicious tongue and was happy to unleash it, particularly on her daughters and daughter-in-laws. Nothing they did was ever good enough, from running the home to cooking, to looking after their children and so on. Her favourite son was Bruno, my dad. She'd encouraged him to take up the reins as head of the household when he was aged only 12, when his father died. They shared a physical similarity, and, as Mum was discovering, a similarly emotional temperament too. Nonna could not believe he'd chosen Elva to be his bride; she was sure Mum must have trapped him. She openly called her an 'English slut' and made sure she felt her disapproval.

It must have been so awful for Mum, facing motherhood so far away from home and with a mother-in-law who held her in contempt. Any comfort she sought from her husband came only on his terms. If she objected to how she was being treated or described how she felt, his temper would first silence her and then he would force her to question whether she was losing her mind. As far as his family was concerned, Bruno was well travelled and charming, a good catch for any woman. Behind closed doors, however, Mum was learning that her worries made her appear only ungrateful in Dad's eyes. He reminded her of her duty, and of all he and his family had done for her. She gave up complaining because the force of his argument left her feeling that she was the one who needed to apologise. Dad could put doubt in anyone's mind and the last thing Mum could risk was falling out with the one person who was there to care for her. Besides, what else could she do? Abroad and isolated, she was trapped.

While my mother's fears grew, Dad revelled in being back home. His mother may have kicked up a fuss about Elva, but his place in her maternal affections hadn't changed. Much to

Mum's relief, however, he did not intend to keep his new bride at his mother's apartment for long and he was looking for a family home. This was the one glimmer of hope for Mum. Each morning she would wake and a lurch of anxiety would hit her as she tiptoed around her mother-in-law, trying her best to stay out of her way. Nonna's life was spent mostly in the kitchen. She would cook and clean furiously, and any woman who didn't do the same was an abomination. But by trying to steer clear of Nonna, Mum was inadvertently adding to her notion that she was a lazy, good-for-nothing. Elva didn't know the first thing about Italian cooking, again, another sign that she was hopeless in Nonna's eyes, but what made her such an easy target was the fact that she could not defend herself verbally. As my mother crept about, Nonna became used to muttering about her in Italian. It only added to her sense that she deserved to be disliked.

Mum threw herself into learning Italian. She knew it was vital if she was ever going to make any friends or find peace of mind in this new country. It's hard to imagine how isolated you can be if you can't speak a language among strangers; it's one thing to greet people and make basic requests, but quite another to establish what kind of person you are; to share jokes and enjoy company if you are not fluent in their language. Dad would speak to Mum in Italian when he was at home and she was lucky to find that one of her sister-in-laws was patient enough to converse with her and correct her mistakes. But it was far from easy and took months, lonely months, as she approached the time her baby was due. On 15 December 1969, Elva was taken to the local hospital and my sister was born the next day, 16 December. She was determined to call her Diana after her best friend, but Dad pointed out that spelt that way it would always be mispronounced as 'Dee-anna'. By adding an extra 'a' before the i, Italians would pronounce the name as we do in English.

Despite the joy she felt at being a mother, returning to Nonna's apartment filled Elva with dread. She was soon criticised for the way she cared for her baby, and although the complaints were completely groundless they were enough to make Mum feel all the more exhausted and depressed by her situation. But within a few months, it looked as if an escape was possible: Dad had found a job in a petro-chemical refinery operated by BP, near Turin. That meant they would have to move and it was a huge move, well over 1,000 km away to the north-west of Italy. Turin is flanked on two sides by the Alps and shares very little with the Mediterranean Italy Dad had grown up with. It can be very cold in the winter and even at the height of summer, temperatures in the hills stay mild. It is also a major industrial and business city, home to big companies such as Fiat, and the wider city has a population over two million – very different from quiet little Brindisi.

Dad didn't plan to move his family into the city but instead found a house some 20 km away: a smallholding in the countryside of Chivasso. It wasn't really a farm, but as with all rural houses then, a small number of animals were kept for the home. This wasn't farming, it was simply what many families did. Having a few pigs, chickens and ducks was a routine part of life: the animals would be reared and then slaughtered when a family occasion required it.

Mum was relieved to be putting some distance between

herself and her mother-in-law, and saw this is as a chance for a fresh start. Dad's attitude towards her was giving her more and more cause for concern. She was scolded for making 'mistakes' and the result was that Dad would be cold and harsh, and days would pass before he accepted her apologies. Mum was sure that once they began their new life beyond the Aggianos in Brindisi, they could start again and enjoy married life. Dad was enthusiastic about the country house: it was the set-up he had imagined for himself, but once they were installed, he expected Mum to cater for him as a traditional Italian wife would. What he hadn't expected was to put up with Mum struggling to adjust to motherhood. He was unsympathetic when it came to her worries and concerns about the baby. To him, this was a natural state of affairs and he had no patience with her tiredness and tears.

Mum loved Daiana from the moment she was put into her arms, but without the support of her own mother or other young mothers like herself to talk to, caring for a baby was sometimes overwhelming. The early months of broken sleep and teething, colds and gripes, left her exhausted. Perhaps Nonna's rantings began to play in the back of Dad's mind because he kept reminding Mum that she had more than a baby to care for; she also had a husband who should come first and a house that needed management. The house should be spotless, laundry washed and ironed, and food prepared. The last thing he would do would be to help out with the baby or with running of the household. He was the man of the house: he should be mum's first concern and she'd just have to try harder.

Mum's hope that the new house would mean a happier home life soon ebbed away: she was told that she was useless. She felt her inadequacies sharply and she would go into her room and cry, wondering how she would ever find the strength to get things right for Bruno. In her eyes, he was right. He had warned her that failing him wasn't just sloppiness, it was sinful; idleness was a sin, as was failing to listen to your husband and submitting yourself to his will.

Talk of sin was never far from Bruno's lips. As Mum was to learn, she wasn't defying Dad, she was transgressing against the word of God by her wilfulness. More than anything, she wanted to make him happy, for him to be pleased with her and to tell her what a good girl she was. After all, as Bruno would point out, he loved her. If she loved him, shouldn't she show it by making him happy? She would try to meet his expectations of how she should behave, what she should wear and even what she should think. Not that he was always unhappy with her. Weeks would pass and then he would be affectionate and loving, reminding her that no one mattered to him as much as she did. He would charm her, 'caress' her, remind her that he thought her beautiful... But when she displeased him, perhaps by not heating his food properly, she would be cast out of his affections and the tension in the household would build again. He would tell her that she was stupid, that she was shameful and slovenly, and so the pattern was set. Without fully realising it, isolated from her family and friends, Mum's character was being slowly dismantled and re-built in the image Dad had created. Elva started to become mindful of what would trigger Bruno's temper; it happened by degrees, and her life began to be run in fear of doing the wrong thing. There was a lot to take on board. If she transgressed, it was best if she admitted her failing. Bruno would point out how he had been provoked and she would promise not to let it happen again and agree that she had been stupid. She had to work harder and surely if she did, she could avoid humiliation and would therefore be loved and back at the heart of his world.

One lifeline proved to be Mum's grasp of Italian. It was the only language she spoke at home now, it was what she spoke to Daiana and she hoped it would help her become more accepted locally. But before too many doubts about her future could settle in, Mum found out she was pregnant again. Daiana was only five months old and by the time she celebrated her first birthday, Mum was approaching full term. My brother, Emmanuele, was born on 21 January 1970.

Dad was thrilled to have a son and even though Mum's workload had more than doubled, he saw no reason not to be entitled to a well-run household. A 1-year-old is exhausting to look after as they are mobile and demanding but coping with a newborn too nearly pushed Mum to the edge. What kept her sane was the time she could enjoy with the children alone. When Emmanuele slept, Mum had the chance to spend time in the garden with Daiana, who would potter about while she picked flowers, enjoyed the sunshine and read to her. She adored her babies, but her life was so much about contrasts. When my dad was happy, he made her the centre of his world, told her that she was his one true love and in his eyes, more beautiful than she'd ever realise, and she would count her blessings. Here she was, with two healthy and beautiful children, far away from the grey skies of home, and with a husband who swore that she was his life. But when Bruno felt she had failed him, her happiness seemed like an illusion. Many hundreds of miles from home, her passport hidden from her, powerless and at his every beck and call, she was his prisoner. What was the reality of her life? The extremes were often more than she could cope with and there were times when she'd sit with Daiana and Emmanuele on her bed and all she could do was weep. There was little chance of visiting home, too. Dad worked hard, but there was never very much money to spare. For now, Elva had to accept her lot, to bring up her children as best she could and to steer them out of the way of Bruno's anger.

Nonna made sure it wasn't too long before she visited her son. What should have surprised and impressed her was how good an Italian cook Mum had become: she loved to cook – it was what was expected of her, but she also excelled at it. She took on board all the basics of how to make the best of Italian cuisine, cooking with the freshest of seasonal produce and allowing simple flavours to come through. Basil, parsley, garlic and olive oil were the building blocks of what became family favourites. Pasta and bread were made at home, and she learned that game and pork dishes were Dad's favourite; anything with pancetta or prosciutto and pasta al forno became her speciality. But no matter how much Mum learned, it failed to impress Nonna. On her visits, she'd make the pasta and produce the meals. Most women would be happy that their mother-in-laws shouldered the burden in the kitchen but of course all this was done within a soured atmosphere: Mum simply wasn't good enough.

When it came to sitting down at mealtimes, Dad would rarely drink alcohol in the house, despite a bottle of red wine being the norm in nearly every other household. He didn't have a taste for it and rarely had alcohol, even at Christmas. He had grown up in Southern Italy where Christmas was remembered for its true meaning and not some gaudy spending spree, but a religious holiday. In December the weather was still mild, and before my mum realised it, the Christmases were ticking by. Her days might seem long, with endless domestic chores to complete, yet time wasn't dragging. There were moments when she doubted she'd get through the day without more tears of frustration, but it seemed that in a blink of an eye Daiana was approaching school age.

The local school wasn't too far, literally a cart ride away. Daiana, and shortly afterwards Emmanuele, were picked up by another family and they would ride in the back of a cart all the way to school. It wasn't remarkable in the region, but it reminded Mum of how little had changed there over the years. Daiana was a proper little Italian girl, bright and easy company. She soon made friends with her classmates and enjoyed mornings at school. She worked hard, and Elva was thrilled to see how much she enjoyed books and finding out more about the world around her.

Emmanuele didn't settle so easily. He could be very rough-and-tumble, loud and boisterous. For him, friendships were harder to form and he often misread how other boys wanted to play and behave. Mum was sure that given time he'd be fine and she'd even started to hope that with more time on her hands at home, she might be able to think about college or finding a part-time job. But it wasn't to be. Dad was adamant her place was at home, and besides, he was thinking of moving again. The family was to be uprooted and to move south again; this time to Caturano, a little village outside the town of Caserta, near Naples, more than 800 km from Turin. Dad had got another job, this time working for the adhesives manufacturer 3M. Mum found herself in a new area, where she knew no one and where there was little chance that her life at home would change.

Around this time, Bruno's interest in religion took a new and sinister twist. He was a very intelligent man who read widely and particularly enjoyed books that suggested that within the Bible there were hidden messages and codes that could be uncovered. Dad knew the Bible intimately. He could quote from it extensively and use passages from it to argue his case, yet somehow his Catholic faith failed to satisfy him entirely. He began to explore other religions, ancient mysticism and even the occult. This was a profound shock for Mum, but there was little she could do and if she ever broached the subject with him, he would be dismissive of her – laugh at her even – and bamboozle her with his knowledge.

Dad was convinced that a different reading of religious texts and a use of mystical and magical techniques could bring him closer to what he was seeking. To Elva's alarm, he even built a makeshift altar, where he'd use incantations, read tarot and burn various 'properties'. It was never clear what these were, but with the incense, the smell was overpowering. He was indifferent to Mum's concerns; she tried to plead with him for their children's sake, but still he carried on. More menacingly, he claimed he was starting to have visions and insights that meant he could see and find things that others could not. He was privileged; mysteries were being revealed to him as he was chosen for his insight. To the outside world, nothing had changed. My dad was a hard worker and good company. He might not stay behind to drink with colleagues or invite them to his home, but if you had questioned any of his workmates, they would only have good things to say about him. And despite this new interest in darker religious forces, day-to-day life at home went on as much as usual. My brother and sister were in no doubt that to stay on the right side of Dad they needed to act straightaway once he had made a request. Any 'naughtiness' was met with a slap from him, but in the 1970s there were very few households that didn't use smacking as part of child discipline.

Life went on, but any ideas Mum might have had about freeing up more time for herself ended in the early summer of 1977 when she realised that she was pregnant again. Dad was happy and Mum knew by now not to expect him to help out with the tasks surrounding childcare. On 18 January 1978, I was born, and soon afterwards christened Natalia Cosima Aggiano. With my arrival came the realisation that we would have to move as extra room was needed to accommodate another child. A house was found in a nearby village called San Marco Evangelista. From the outset Mum's new daughter was far more restless than her first born. I was a livewire, happy when I was occupied with something to distract me, but a real handful whenever I was bored. Daiana, now 9 years old, was expected to help out with the household and childcare. If Mum was occupied with me cooking, then it was her job to keep me out of mischief.

It can't have been easy for my sister, but Dad made sure that she realised it was expected of her. As he'd grown up, daughters were left in no doubt that they had to shoulder household chores alongside their mothers and that meant caring for the male members of the family, too. It's hard to understand now, but then sisters were expected to wait hand and foot not just on their fathers but their brothers. This was how Dad had grown up and not only did he make sure that this was still the case when Daiana was growing up in Italy, it was an attitude he maintained even when I was growing up in the UK. Daiana was at an age when she realised that despite the outward façade, things at home were far from happy. To Dad, the household was run just as it should be but she was old enough to note how often Mum closed the door of her bedroom and sobbed. Not that she could challenge Dad. His temper was terrifying and she too was made to feel a failure in his eyes. He'd delight in telling her that she was not as clever as him, as good-looking or worthy of respect. Any achievements at school were dismissed. If she got three As, Dad sneered about missing out on four. It was corrosive, and any attempts Daiana made to build her self-esteem were stamped on.

When I was around 2 years old, Nonna came to visit. She wasn't happy with the way Elva was keeping house and attacked her for spending time on the sofa reading books with her children. For once, Mum held strong and said, 'The children will remember that I made time to read to them. That will be more important than how many times I washed the floor in one day.' And she was right. But Nonna saw this as more reason to distrust Mum and she knew how to create a foul atmosphere by saying hateful things. At the time, Dad used to drive a small yellow Fiat. One day I was looking out of the window while Daiana watched over me.

I was suddenly excited and shouted: 'Yellow car! yellow car – it's daddy!'

Nonna shot back, 'Well, it *might* be.'

No doubt she was again introducing the idea that Mum was a loose woman who'd trapped Dad and that we were all probably illegitimate. Daiana was only 11, but understood the remark well enough. Her life was far from easy: at school she was used to being reminded that she had an 'English mother' and was made to feel an outsider, but to hear acidic remarks from her own grandmother too cut far deeper.

Events at home were soon overtaken by fears for Emmanuele's health, though quite suddenly, at the age of 10, he had a seizure. It was terrifying for Mum and she feared the worst. One fit was followed by another and another, and they were far more severe than anything Mum had experienced as a child, who used to zone out for a minute or so, unable to focus or tune in to what was going on around her. Doctors diagnosed epilepsy and my parents worried constantly about how Emmanuele would cope. What if he was alone and swallowed his tongue? What if he had a fit in the night and choked on his own vomit? It was every parent's nightmare and added an additional strain to the household.

But in the summer of 1981, the family was to take a holiday that would change everything. Finally, Mum was able to return to stay with her family. We arrived in Cleethorpes and despite it being July, the weather was typically poor. It was so much cooler than Italy, and Mum and Dad noticed that Emmanuele's condition improved enormously. Back in Italy, doctors confirmed that they thought a cooler climate would be better for his health. And so, in November 1981, the Aggiano family travelled back to England, this time, for good.

CHAPTER THREE

A NEW LIFE

I don't have any memories of arriving in England. It's a shame as it must have been so different from Italy, but I was not yet 3 years old and so I can't remember life in those first few weeks at my Aunty Jean's.

Families pull together in times of need and I'm sure Mum appreciated her sister's invitation to stay with her, but with three children underfoot, it can't have been easy. Mum and Dad were grateful as they'd arrived back in Scunthorpe lock, stock and barrel, with no accommodation arranged for our family of five. In fact, they had little choice but to live with relatives – money was tight, they had limited savings and so they couldn't afford to rent a home until Bruno found work.

Schooling had to be sorted out for my brother and sister, but I was still young enough to stay home with Mum. Dad's first priority was to get a job. Throughout his life, he had been very hardworking and so he was confident that with the experience he had working in heavy industry and manufacturing, it shouldn't be too difficult. His English was good, but his accent clearly pointed out his origins, and yet he never felt that this held him back. In the meantime, Mum registered the family with the local council and our names were placed on a waiting list for a house. Daiana and Emmanuele must have had a shock to find themselves in a school environment where only English was spoken. To hear Daiana now, you would never think she spent much of her childhood in Italy; she has no trace of an accent but she can still speak Italian fluently. With Emmanuele, you'd never believe that he did most of his growing up here; his Italian accent is still very strong, but if you sat down and talked to me, you'd be sure I was a girl born and bred on Humberside.

It's hard for me to believe now that back then, at 3 years old, I didn't have a word of English. Mum began using English with me, to help me become fully adjusted to our new life, and any doubts she might have had about the language switch were dropped after one incident. Needing to sort out the house move, they left me with one of my mum's friends for the morning. Unable to speak a word of English, I started saying '*acqua, acqua*'. My mum's friend had no idea what I was asking for. She handed over toys, walked me about to try and distract me but it was clear that I was getting more and more distressed. She thought I must be missing Mum and so was relieved when my parents knocked on the door to pick me up. Mum heard me cry '*acqua*' and said, 'She's asking for water, she's thirsty.' From that day on, she only spoke to me in English at home.

In one way, it's a shame because I can't speak Italian. Mum and Dad still used both languages to each other and Dad would often say things to me in his native tongue –I'd usually understand what he was asking but as time went on, it was as if that part of my heritage became lost to me. Yet Dad continued to talk to me in Italian, and near the end of his life, all the more so. I couldn't reply in Italian but it remained a vital link between us.

Not that I realised any of this as a rowdy toddler. All I cared about was based around me, my mum and dad, brother and sister. I was the baby and could expect lots of attention from Mum. I was a bit of a handful, though, and not easy to distract when it came to Mum's attempts to cook and get on with the housework.

I hated to see her go into the kitchen as I knew that meant no time for her to play with me. And I never thought to involve Dad in play – it was just something that he'd never do. I honestly don't think he knew how to play with his children. I don't know if this was because he felt it wasn't what men did, or because he himself had never been played with when he was growing up, but whatever the reason, I don't think he would have known where to start. What he would do, though, was put me on his shoulders whenever we went out for walks, perhaps to see the Humber Bridge, and I loved that. I can remember one walk we took when Mum tried to point out a boat on the river for me to see. I kept saying, 'Where, where?' I was looking out to the water but my mum's hand was on the hood of my coat and she was holding it in such a way that it came down to my nose, covering my eyes entirely. It was only when she looked down that she realised. To this day, I can remember her laughing and it is one of the happiest times I can recall as a child, with both Mum and Dad enjoying time as a family.

We didn't go on days out very often. Mostly, at home the day's routine was the same. Once Dad came home, the whole household would shift to putting him at its centre. Whether he wanted a cup of coffee, food, to talk or preferred to have the kids out of the room so he could have peace and quiet, his mood dictated exactly what would happen. It was just something I took for granted, seeing Mum's harried face as she rushed about, making sure the household met Dad's expectations. Although I don't have any memories of my first few months in England, I do remember moving into our new house. It was a council house on the outskirts of Scunthorpe in a district called Westcliffe. The house was great. It meant a new start for us all, and I can remember being excited as we moved our boxes in and realised that we had three whole floors and a garden at the back to ourselves.

It must have been a huge relief to Elva. She wasn't willing to talk about the state of her marriage to her sister Jean – I don't think she knew how to approach the subject and had spent the last few months trying to keep up appearances. Now at least she could close the door and know she was in her own home. Unfortunately, the same was true for Dad. Once more, he expected the household to be run in his way. The good news was that he had found work by setting up a stall selling clothes in the local market; the bad news was that the cost of living in Scunthorpe was much higher than in Italy and money would remain tight. Mum was always good at keeping to a budget, but she knew that money worries would not help improve the atmosphere at home. Yet she kept reminding Dad why they were back in England: that it was for the good of Emmanuele's health and that they were seeing real benefits. His fits were not so frequent and he was able to go to school and work hard. Emmanuele loved books almost as much as his dad so they had high hopes of him.

I was never close to my brother. I don't know if it was the age difference, but he just didn't have much time for me and, in some ways, we were always strangers. We just never seemed on the same wavelength. As the boy of the house, he could expect Mum and Daiana to run around for him and I think part of me, even when I was tiny, resented this.

I was much closer to Daiana. Once she was home and Mum needed to get to work in the kitchen, so she had to mind me. She was incredibly responsible even at a young age. I could see that she worked hard to stay on the right side of Dad as his temper could be so bad. Dad thought nothing of lashing out and smacking if he thought he'd been disobeyed, but in truth it was his shouting that could do most damage, causing genuine terror in us all. Daiana had learned that the easiest way to shelter from him was to do as he said.

It was so tough on her. At thirteen, she was much older than me but wasn't allowed to go and visit friends or have friends over and she certainly wasn't allowed to go to any after-school clubs or wear make-up or fashionable clothes. She was dressed so conservatively that she could be mistaken for a middle-aged woman from behind. Now, I find it incredible to realise that Mum too was dressed far beyond her years – after all, she was only just into her thirties. She was in the prime of life and should have felt so, but Dad kept her in long skirts and long-sleeved tops, so she rarely looked anything but dowdy.

But this wasn't something she fought against because she was very self-conscious about the way she looked. When she was unhappy, she'd turn to food and comfort eat. Over the years, this meant she put on quite a lot of weight. She hated to catch sight of herself in the mirror but the more unhappy her shape made her, the more she seemed to find relief in food. The relief wouldn't last either. She'd soon feel guilty and so she was stuck in the cycle of bingeing and shame about what she was doing. Her real weakness was fried food – chocolate and sweet stuff never tempted her in the way that savoury food could.

In the kitchen, Mondays to Fridays were devoted to Italian food but even then, if she made a calzone – a sort of pizza folded in half – she would finish cooking it in the deep-fat fryer. Her other treat was chips and fried eggs, a meal she would make at any time of the day in addition to the family meal she'd already prepared. A man would deliver a huge bag of potatoes at the start of the week and it would always be empty by the end. On Saturdays and Sundays, the kitchen was given over to English food, which meant a full English breakfast on Saturday mornings, and on Sundays a traditional roast dinner with all the trimmings.

On Sundays, of course, we'd have to go to church. So Mum would get up at 6am to prepare the food. Other than cooking, her only other outlet was church. The same was true of my sister – at a time when she should have been at youth clubs or out with friends, she'd be expected to go to church meetings. Little did I know what impact this was to have on our lives. Dad's interest in the occult had waned since his arrival in England, but his need to immerse himself in religious texts had not. More and more, he started to believe that there were hidden mathematical codes in the Bible, and somehow this led to a new interest in the Jehovah's Witnesses. Their teachings include a belief in 'End Times'– that only 144,000 people will become the 'anointed' and will ascend and be chosen to rule in the Kingdom of Heaven with Christ. The countdown to the End Times is said to have already begun, revealed by interpreting significant dates in the Bible. Dad decided that this was a faith worth adhering to and told Mum that the family would now start to attend Jehovah's meetings.

Now I realise how much of the beliefs of the Jehovah's Witnesses blended with Dad's particular view of the world. Homosexuality is an abomination, abortion is wrong and gender roles are strictly defined: a wife must serve her husband, she must act as a loving caretaker, assisting her husband in his role as head of the household. The Jehovahs, like Dad, believed in Satan and his demons too; that we are all exposed to suffering since Eve's betrayal in the Garden of Eden, and by not following Jehovah's teachings, we leave ourselves open to illness and disease. The 'witnessing' comes from the need to show your faith in and obedience to God and Jesus Christ as Lord and Saviour, and demonstrating obedience certainly appealed to Dad. Another strand is the certainty that other Christians have deviated from the true teachings of the Bible and that it is right to ignore their 'human speculation' and 'contaminated creed'. Dad spent much of his life feeling that he was right and most other people were wrong. With the backing of faith, he felt righteous when he decided how to organise his household. So what if other men let their wives do as they pleased? Most men might think this was OK but Dad's need to keep us on a leash wasn't ever going to be about his own shortcomings – after all, he was simply acting out the dictates of his faith and God himself, or so he believed.

Dad would read the Bible in Italian and English, and instruct us to sit and listen as he read out passages he felt passionately about. It was easy for someone with his outlook to see more in the text than at first reading. For example, Psalm 32:8: 'I shall make you have insight and instruct you in the way you should go. I will give advice with my eye upon you'. Later, Dad's belief that he had a special mission and special instructions while on earth would grow stronger. The 'eye was upon him', but it was on us, too, directed through Dad.

It was all heavy stuff – this talk of sin and Satan and redemption – but at the time, I remember very little other than thinking that sitting in church, attending group meetings and knocking on doors was perfectly normal, if dull. But I think for Daiana, a teenager at the time, this must have increased her sense of isolation from her classmates all the more, particularly as we were now no longer to celebrate Christmas, Easter or birthdays, which was something that marked you out as different – and as a kid, different is never good.

I had no true idea how different my home life was to that of the children around me, but as I got ready for my first day at school, I didn't feel anxious. All I felt was excitement. I just couldn't wait to start and the only tears shed on that first day were Mum's. That morning, she thought she was waving goodbye to her last child starting school so she had mixed feelings. Yes, it meant that she had more time to herself but it was still a wrench.

School was fun. I loved making new friends, some of whom lived close to our house in Westcliffe. We'd walk the same route home and I was allowed to play at their homes provided Mum came along too and we were home in time to prepare Dad's tea. I could have friends over, too, and loved to run and climb up the stairs because there were just so many of them. I loved the top floor of the house because as well as my mum and dad's bedroom, there was a room with rails of clothes for Dad's market stall – real treasures, I thought, as I ran my hand through them.

In many respects, I thought life at this time was good, but I later learned that it was because Mum was shielding me from so much. Daiana knew that if she got on the wrong side of Dad, Mum would suffer too. This was something I didn't know. And if I was bad, I would be hit, but Mum would be subject to Dad's verbal attacks. She would be told that she was a bad mother, that she had let her daughter become disrespectful and that my wickedness was a result of her sinfulness. I thought nothing of being slapped: I would cry in my room and watch the handprint rise red on the back of my leg, but I never questioned why Dad thought it was OK to use violence to discipline us. After a while, Mum would come and open the door to my room and lead me quietly to the kitchen, where she'd give me a snack and urge me to eat quietly.

Whatever misery Mum endured she'd try to hide it and she'd attempt to distract herself and relearn the teachings of the Bible, when there was much about the burden of unhappiness and about life being fleeting. The task was to obey her God and try to live well. Not that she was lost in spiritual contemplation. To meet her, she was just like every other mum at the school gate. Her faith was important to her as I truly think it helped her endure the darker moments of her marriage and I think knocking on doors cost her a lot. Her faith was private: she was never zealous and the idea of crusading to convert people would not have sat easily with her. I think she was just doing as she was told when it came to being a Jehovah's Witness. She didn't dislike people who didn't believe, and would never dream of condemning them, but Dad ringfenced the people she was allowed to talk to and that meant friendships were only possible with people in the church. What was the alternative? If she didn't go to church I don't think she would have been allowed to talk to anyone outside the house at all.

Throughout her life, Mum was down to earth; she was grounded in the day-to-day and had simple aspirations, too. One of her dreams was for herself and Bruno to own their own home. Dad had stopped working on the stall as a job had come up at a plastic bag factory and that meant a guaranteed full-time wage, something more reliable than the stall. A full-time job also meant that they could raise a mortgage. Buying a home must have been what Dad wanted too or it would never have happened, and so they began to look around to see what was available. In 1985, they put down a small deposit on a three-bedroom terraced house in Old Crosby in Scunthorpe. Mum was really pleased to be moving into a house that we could call our own. It was a simple home, where the yards at the rear backed onto what we called the '10 foot', an alleyway that ran between the houses – the perfect place for the kids to pour into and play safely. I loved it. Even though it meant moving to a new school, we'd arrived during the summer holidays and I'd had a chance to make friends before the school year began.

My school was a few minutes' walk away and life would have been easy if it hadn't been for Dad's deteriorating state of mind. It is this house, the house in which Mum would meet her terrible death, that harbours most of the misery I was to face over the next ten years. Even now, I can't look at pictures showing the brown sofa we had or the pale blue patterned wallpaper without thinking of what I was subjected to. The problem, I was told, was me. The older I got, the harder I found it not to stand up to Dad. When we moved in, I was only 7, and so a smack across the legs was usually all it took to make me comply. But as the years passed, I was the one who'd answer him back and pay the consequences. My defiance was met with increasing levels of physical violence, yelling gave way to slapping and then to punches. My 'disrespect' led to an underlying tension in the household and sporadic outbreaks of violence as Dad attempted to assert his control over me. These episodes came to scar my childhood. I can remember coming home one afternoon after school and Dad telling me, 'Go and make me a cup of coffee.' It was the kind of casual order that he didn't think twice about giving so when I replied with, 'No! You go – you've got legs, haven't you?', all hell broke loose.

Dad hurled me from the room, hitting and kicking me as I crawled towards the stairs. He punched me in the ribs and I can remember being doubled up with the pain. But despite the agony I was in, I couldn't bring myself to apologise, even as the blows came down on me and I stumbled towards my room, tears streaming down my face. I lay on my bed sobbing and the one consolation was that he would have to get someone else to make his coffee. Daiana could do it if she wanted. Not me. Those kind of beatings were not unusual. The bruises would be confined to my body; it was very rare that he'd make the mistake of hitting me in the face. Mum would plead with me not to make Dad cross. She could sense the tension building between us and knew that Dad needed no more than a spark of anger from me for his temper to go up like tinder. She would urge me just to do as I was told, but as time passed, I would taunt her: 'I don't care, I hate him. I wish he was dead.' My anger would wash over how I felt about Mum too. How *could* she put up with him?

But it seemed there was no escape from Dad. I started to fantasise that I was adopted and that my real parents would arrive and I could finally escape him. For the time being, my escape was school. From time to time, I'd be asked by friends about my bruises, but I didn't know what to say. I felt a burning shame and didn't want to tell them that my dad hated me so much he'd drag me from the room by my hair, screaming at me. Then something happened to him that had a big impact at home. At work in the carrier-bag factory, he picked up a huge bale of plastic meant for two men He was frustrated that the man he was working alongside was so slow and moved it himself. The result was massive damage to his back: He was in agony and ended up having to be signed off sick. Back home, this was a catastrophe: we'd lost Dad's income and he was confined to the house. Now there was no escape from his tyranny, and the fact that he couldn't work made his moods all the more bitter.

It was around this time that a police officer came into school. I loved it when we had visits in school as it meant time away from our desks. The talk he gave was pretty routine stuff about safety in and outside the home, but then during question time, I can remember he started to talk about smacking. He said that parents had to teach children the difference between right and wrong, but that hitting wasn't really right. Without thinking, I said, 'My mum hit me with a wooden spoon.' The stupid thing was, it was the only time she'd ever hit me. She was trying to get food ready for 5pm, the time Dad expected his plate to be put in front of him. I was acting up and I don't remember exactly why, but she snapped. She picked up her spoon and whacked the back of my leg. It didn't really hurt. I think I remembered it so clearly as it was such an odd thing for Mum to do. But once I said it out loud in class, I regretted it. Straightaway, I could tell that I couldn't take it back. I was taken outside to the corridor, where I started to worry that

I had done something wrong. The policeman asked me again and I said that Mum had only done it once.

'What about your dad?' asked the policeman.

'He hits me a lot. A lot with his fists,' I told him.

I was taken back to class and a teacher walked me home at the end of the day. I was scared and was right to be so as the police had called home the same day. I was petrified of Dad. Straightaway, Mum told the teacher that it wasn't true, that I had a rich imagination and that she was sorry I'd wasted everyone's time. It was no more than I expected of her, to side with Dad, but when my teacher left and Mum asked me why I had said what I did, I replied, 'Because you told me never to lie.' Mum gave Dad a sharp look, something she would never usually do. And Dad said nothing at all. He sat there, and I went to bed, relieved I'd avoided punishment.

But the incident wasn't over yet. A social worker visited home and told Mum that I would have to see a child psychologist and then attend sessions about once a month. What's more, the whole family was called in for a meeting. What a farce that must have been! We were all decked out in our Sunday best and I can remember hardly saying a word. Then I was taken to a room and asked to draw a picture. I wanted to know what I was to draw. Anything you like, I was told. All I could manage was a few stick men and a house. At later sessions, I was asked to play with two dolls or look at cards and say what I thought the squiggles meant. 'A squiggle,' I'd answer.

It didn't help. There was absolutely no way I felt comfortable enough to talk to these strangers about life at home and I had no way of explaining what shame and turmoil my dad's violence made me feel. I just knew I had to say nothing or I'd put Mum in danger. Mum had been wracked with nerves over the intervention of the social workers and pleaded with me not to try and get Dad into trouble as she was terrified that the family would be split up. Yet any suspicions the school or social workers may have failed to stop Dad. At home, I'd say something cheeky and he would take his frustration out on me, hitting me. He'd make sure I'd cry – he needed to see me break before he'd stop. I kept silent throughout my sessions with the psychologist; they left me feeling ashamed. It never felt like a lifeline or as if I was being offered the hope that things could be different; it just added to my sense that things were wrong at home and I hated to be singled out in this way. I thought the tests and discussions were stupid and a waste of time; the grown-ups were trying to catch me out and my misgivings caused me to withdraw into myself. I couldn't bear to be examined by people I was unable to trust. Instead, I buried much of what was happening during those years. Much later, I found something I'd written on a torn-out piece of paper from an exercise book. It was a poem I'd found, and as I read through it, tears of recognition streamed down my face. Here's part of it:

Why is Daddy mad?
I tried so hard today
To do everything he wanted
And to stay out of his way
I feel bad that daddy

From God was given me
He wanted a child
He could be proud of
Not me as I can clearly see
I don't understand it
Mummy says she loves me too
But when daddy hits me
She says there is nothing she can do.

I didn't know who wrote it, but I often wondered about their life. On one level, it made me realise that I was not the only child suffering at home behind closed doors. On another, it made me wonder why it would not stop, why I was always thought of as so bad – bad enough for the man who should be caring for me to hit and want to hurt me. All I wanted was my dad to be like the other dads I saw, happy and loving; I just wanted a normal life.

Time and again, I'd ask Mum to leave him but she'd say that she couldn't. Later, I learned that she had even been to see her GP and asked if there was something he could do. She asked if there was psychiatric help available for Bruno as more than anyone, she sensed that his rage had to have a root in unhappiness or some sort of twisted need to dominate. But she was turned down, with the GP stating that Dad himself would have to come to the surgery and ask for help. That, of course, was out of the question and heaven knows what would have happened to Mum if he had found out that the reason behind her visit to the doctor was to talk about him. In his eyes, he was doing what he was entitled to; keeping Mum and me in our place.

At home, life was made all the harder when there was so little money to spare. As well as the air of menace, I felt that I was missing out on all the toys my friends had – their bedrooms seemed packed with toys compared to mine. I hated not having the toys other kids had; I wanted a cabbage patch doll and a glow worm and a Barbie, but there was no way. Sometimes, we'd be taken to jumble sales where I'd get a lot of my clothes, unless Mum had made them – she was very talented when it came to knitting and sewing. I do remember Dad buying me a dolls' house for 50p at one jumble sale, but I had no dolls to put inside; I'd make paper ones or use my finger instead. They were never very good, but if I complained, Dad told me I was greedy, wicked and selfish. And, of course, there were no birthdays or Christmases to look forward to as they were banned by our faith.

Tension rose even more when Mum suggested to Dad that she should try and find work. Her dream was to go to college and gain a nursing qualification. Dad railed against this, insisting Mum was where she should be. Mum said that her studies wouldn't interfere with the smooth running of the home as she'd be sure to be back in time to fix food and finish any laundry or cleaning. She also pointed out that we children were old enough not to need her to stay at home and that she'd always be home in time to let me in from school anyway. What she was suggesting enraged him; he said it was her way of trying to flaunt herself in front of men. I can remember Mum's tears, but I can also remember how hard I was, even at 9. 'Just leave him, Mum. We all hate him. Let's just go!' But still she said nothing.

The only time I could get her to talk about leaving was whenever I'd been in trouble with Dad and once again been beaten. She would come and see me and I'd beg her to leave. 'When you are 18,' she'd tell me and smooth my hair, 'then I can leave.' I don't know how she managed it, but she did at last start her nursing course. I remember all her coursework on the dining-room table but there was never a time she wasn't in when we were at home. Her studying went really well – she was getting great marks and clearly enjoying the chance to use her intelligence. Then, out of the blue, Mum told us she was pregnant. Looking back, it seems all too convenient that she fell pregnant at the very time when she was quietly trying to get Dad to see the sense of her gaining her nursing qualification. Years later, Dad told me that he had deliberately got her pregnant, but back then, there was no hint of anything of that kind. I'm sure Mum must have had her doubts.

I was excited that Mum was going to have another baby but too young to realise that this meant that she was once again fully in Dad's control. The household settled down again as we waited for the new arrival, with Mum more cautious than ever not to anger Dad and even I made sure not to cross him. In September 1987, Daniel was born, and I was thrilled, as was the whole family. But the little boy who'd become the main object of all my love and affection had to learn to suffer too. He was born into a world that would violently fall apart, and he was to be effectively orphaned, before he'd even reached the age of 10.

CHAPTER FOUR

TEEN SPIRIT

It's strange that one of my fondest memories of Elva was of waking up at night during a terrible thunderstorm. I was 10 years old and lay in bed listening as the rain lashed down; I remember the lightening illuminating the staircase for a split second as I crept downstairs. It was one moment held, with all the colours of the hallway lit, as I stood in my pyjamas and held onto the banister before being swallowed back into the darkness.

I had woken up as I sensed Mum was up, and she was. She was sitting in an armchair, heavily pregnant, watching the storm. Calling me over, I sat next to her and she put my hands on her stomach. As the thunder cracked, the baby would kick. 'That's your baby brother,' she said. I felt so at peace sitting next to Mum but told her firmly: 'No, it's a sister, not a brother. If it's a boy, I'm running away!' She just smiled and smoothed my hair, and we sat together until the storm had passed.

A few days later Dad woke me up and said that Mum had gone into hospital and that the baby had been born. I was confused as I was sure Mum was still in the house. She had put me to bed the night before so I thought he had got it wrong. But she wasn't there and Dad picked me up after school to take me to the hospital. I'd been grumpy all day, sorely disappointed that Mum had gone ahead and done what I'd told her not to and had a boy. Arriving at hospital, Daniel was put in my arms and all my annoyance melted away; in fact, everything changed. I loved him to distraction. Once again, it was Daiana who had to shoulder the burden of childcare and more household chores while I could just breeze in and play with my little brother. He was a joy. He soon grew a mop of gorgeous curls and had the most infectious laugh I'd ever heard. I made a fuss of him, dressed him up, hid him in my room, and all together thought him the best thing that had ever happened to me. Yet I was growing up in a household where to show that you were in charge, you used violence. It makes me sick to my stomach to think about it now but when Daniel got on my nerves or grabbed something I was playing with, I'd lash out. I thought nothing of hitting him and pushing him violently. To me, this was normal – Mum would say, 'Not his face. If you have to hit him, hit his legs.'

What still makes me shudder to this day is that I would take him to my room, lie him on my bed and put a pillow over his face. I would then make cackling noises and he'd be truly terrified. Satisfied he was crying with fear, I'd rush over and scoop him up, telling him, 'Don't worry, the witch is gone – it's OK now.' I loved to comfort him; to let him know that it was going to be alright. Even as a tiny baby, I'd poke him when he was asleep just so I could rock him back to sleep again.

The poor boy had no peace from me. I'd raid Daiana's clothes and shoes and then dress him in them, treating him like my plaything. My other joy was watching a copy of *Annie* on video. Daniel would sit next to me and soon learned to join in with 'It's a Hard Knock Life'. I was sure I was an orphan like Annie and lived her every misery. At school, I'd invent stories too, insisting I was adopted or about to leave and live somewhere else. My one outlet in school was drama, easily my favourite lesson. I welcomed the chance to be someone else and it was the only time I was truly happy as the other me was folded away.

My life at home left me angry and confused, and school became a natural escape as it meant being with people who knew nothing about my life with my parents. I found making friends easy enough and I would go to their houses but I was wary about people coming home with me. I wasn't sure what they would think, whether they'd guess something wasn't right and I would be humiliated in some way.

I had made one close friend in a girl called Helen. We'd sit and giggle and she was as bad as me at avoiding schoolwork at all costs. I made every effort in class to fool around. I wasn't going to be like Daiana: she was smart, excelled at school and had found a good job. She was the golden girl and I wasn't going to be a bookworm like her, just to please Dad. I'd even gone as far as to choose a different secondary school from my sister. I went to Foxhills, which suited me well enough although I never found I could concentrate on my schoolwork. I'd struggle with Maths in particular. Dad, who was incredibly smart when it came to anything to do with numbers, would try and instruct me. 'I don't get it,' I'd say, with my best pre-teen bored look. It would drive him crazy of course. But I wanted nothing from him, or at least that's what I thought. I couldn't stand him, I hated him. In fact, in moments of rage after he'd hit me, I wanted to find out if there was a way I could kill him. That way, we'd all be free.

Ideas of death had begun to settle in me since just before Daniel had been born, when my grandfather died. My dad took me to see him in his coffin, one day after school. As I looked down on him, I kept staring at the hairs up his nose and whispered to Dad, 'You've got to be careful, he's going to wake up.' Dad told me he'd never wake up, that once you were dead, you were dead for good and nothing could bring you back. It stayed with me and in my mind, I dreamt that Dad would go too and not wake up.

I didn't know how it came about but an opportunity presented itself. One place Dad was happy was at his allotment – he'd grow vegetables and spend hours digging over the soil. There was a small shed and he'd found evidence that rats had been there, so he bought some rat poison pellets and then kept what he hadn't used under the sink. I found them and read how toxic they were. One Saturday afternoon, he told me yet again to make him some coffee and so I did. I put pellets of rat poison in it, carefully stirring until they dissolved. With my heart pounding, I brought the coffee into the front room and handed the mug to him. He took one sip and spat it out, saying the milk must be off. I was told to open a new bottle of milk and make a fresh cup. He never found out that this was my first attempt to kill him.

The older I got, more and more points of conflict came up between us. By now, I had become an expert liar. Of course this was all driven by a desperation to get him out of my life and sometimes it would backfire badly. There was a girl, Emma, living on the same street as us that I got on well with. Her mum was divorced, and so in Dad's eyes, she was a fallen woman. He told me I was not to play with her, that her mother's sinfulness would contaminate Emma and me. I swore to him that I wouldn't, but secretly, I would still knock on her door – I was sure he wouldn't find out. Despite having few toys, one thing I did have was a bike as Dad was still passionate about cycling. Oddly, despite so many restrictions on what I could do, I was always allowed to go for a bike ride. So one afternoon, I lied about who I was calling for and instead rode off to see Emma. What I didn't realise was that Dad had gone out to the local shop and on his return, had watched me riding my bike alongside Emma. When I got back, he called out asking where I'd been. Out came my cover story and he rushed at me with such speed that my back was still turned as he came into the kitchen. He grabbed me from behind, dragging me by the hair. I screamed but no one came. He told me he would beat me for my lying and he was true to his word, punching hard into my back and ribs.

I remember curling up in a ball in my room crying. Daniel, still a tiny child, came in and wiped away my tears and whispered to me that we could run away together. But what could we do? Mum wouldn't leave. She now told me that was only possible when Daniel reached 18. So I told her that I now hated her too; that she was evil to bring me into this family, that it was her fault for being so selfish in wanting me and that I hated being alive. She looked upset but did nothing; she didn't even fight back. It was around this time that I started stealing from her. We had so little to spare but I would take change and pounds when I felt like it. I never spent it on myself, on the many things I wanted. Instead, I'd give it to friends or buy sweets and give them away. Mum would call me into the kitchen and ask me about the money missing from her purse. I'd look straight into her eyes and say, 'On my life, Mum, I swear I haven't.' I wanted her to know I was lying, that I could do what I wanted, that she was weak in my eyes...

I was 14 when Daiana left home. As far as I could see, she had accepted the first offer of marriage that came along and I could hardly blame her. I remember her bringing her fiancé home and how I took an instant dislike to him. Daiana and I weren't close, but I sat on the stairs and asked her not to marry him, pleading with her that he wasn't nice. But once she left, it was a long time before I gave her life some thought. At this age, I was existing at a point where caring about myself, and occasionally Daniel, was about all I could manage. In practical terms, Daiana's leaving meant the good news that I had a room to myself, a room that I holed up in more and more. I was pleased to find that she had left a little portable kettle in the room too as that would mean even less need to go downstairs. Mum would lecture me and sometimes grow cross as I 'treated the house like a hotel' but I didn't care. They could all go to hell as far as I was concerned.

Inevitably, I took up smoking. Mum would give me a £1 for lunch money and I would spend 99p on fags. I knew my dad would hate it; neither of them had ever smoked. I used to have this bizarre 'what if' ritual with Dad.

'What would you do if you found out I was smoking Dad?'

'I'd make you eat a packet of cigarettes until you threw them up,' he'd say.

For some reason, I liked the game and I would raise the stakes.

'What if you found out I was pregnant, Dad?'

'You would keep the baby, of course. But I would find the man and beat him severely,' was his reply.

'What would you do if I was raped, Dad?'

'I would find the man and I would kill him with my own hands.'

And so it would go on. I would ask questions of the big bad wolf and he would tell me about what blood sacrifice each sin would demand. Sin was everywhere, and Dad reminded us all the time that he was ever-vigilant, and that we should be glad that he was. It was a great irony to me that Dad's religious faith frowned on unchaperoned 'dates', something he wholeheartedly applauded, but was also disapproving of 'fits of anger' and 'violence', something he himself seemed to take or leave. I would provoke him with questions because I liked to hear that if I was the victim of an attack or a badly-behaved boyfriend, Dad would rouse himself into a fury and avenge me. It meant that I was important to him in some way after all; that even though I was the badly-behaved daughter, never the shining star Daiana promised to be, if there was a transgression, he would rush out and fight for me. It was one of the few times he seemed to show that he cared about me. What I hadn't taken on board fully was that he cared about my reputation, wanting to make sure my conduct did not dishonour him and his name: monitoring me wasn't love, it was control.

His need to control spilled into every area of my life. A vest top would be banned from my wardrobe as it meant that I 'was asking for it'. When my periods started, I had to use sanitary towels, which I hated, and not Tampax, as all my friends did, because to use one would mean that I had been penetrated and was no longer a virgin. No, I was not to go on a weekend break with my friend as her father would take the opportunity to rape me. It was made clear to me that nowhere was safe except under his careful eye. So smoking was a risk but at least one that would only mean a punishment that involved vomit and confinement to my room. And smoke I would, usually out of my window. One rainy and blustery day, I climbed inside my wardrobe with a can to stub out the cigarette when I heard Mum coming up the stairs and heading for my room. There was smoke billowing out from under the wardrobe door, but when she pulled it open she found me looking at her with an air of innocence.

She demanded, 'Have you been smoking?'

'No,' I said coldly, 'absolutely not.'

I stared at her longer than she stared at me so that she'd know that she'd have to back down and let me get away with it.

I hated that Mum had started to be wary of me, that she'd

look at me out of the corner of her eye, weighing up what I was going to do next, wondering how to intervene before I could shatter any peace in the house. She'd learnt the hard way that I had a mind of my own and could be pig-headed when I wanted to be. When I was 8, I told her I didn't like my long hair anymore. I told her to cut it, but she refused; I told her to take me to the hairdressers, but she said no to that, too. So I told her that I would get the scissors myself and hack it off. Mum knew by looking at me that I would do so, no matter how much she hoped I wouldn't and so I had my hair cut really short. I looked like a boy, and was even mistaken for a boy sometimes, but that suited me just fine. I was always something of a tomboy and yet I treated Daniel as a doll, constantly making him pretty when I myself wouldn't go near girlie stuff. That was changing the older I got, but Mum learnt that the one thing that wouldn't change was my stubbornness.

One breakthrough for Mum eventually came out of an ongoing worry for Dad. Money was always tight and things had got to the point that when Elva was offered a job as a receptionist in a local JCB plant, he allowed her to take it – but with restrictions. It was farcical. He would walk her to work, pick her up and stay with her during her lunch break. This was to stop her talking to the male members of staff. Any other woman would have laughed at the idea of being chaperoned by a jailer of a husband but I knew she had no other choice but to go along with it if she expected to have a life outside the house at all. The knock-on effect for me was that I was expected to come home and make Dad's tea for 5pm. With no Daiana, it was all down to me and became a new point of conflict. One evening, I burnt his food deliberately. Dad knew straightaway and hurled himself at me. He forgot his golden rule and hit me in the face as well as my ribs. My face was swollen and bruised, and Mum was horrified. She kept me off school for two days. On the third day, I had to go back to school and tell everyone that I had fallen down the stairs.

One break time, it all got too much and I broke down in tears in the toilets. The friend who found me pleaded with me to tell a teacher, and so I did. The teacher said, 'Well, it's a bit late now to do anything!' Part of me broke. There would be no end to this. Dad could do what he liked, and in the end, there was no one who could help me. But a call from school was made to home. Again, Mum said I was lying. When I got home, she took me aside and said that if I ever did that again, it would not be Dad who'd be taken away but Daniel. That was the one thing that would guarantee my silence and now it breaks my heart to think that she knew that. But this wasn't the first time Mum had had to cover up for Dad. How many more times would she do so, putting him before me or Daniel before something changed? To me, it was always the wrong things that changed.

Once, when Dad had lost his temper he had dragged me through the kitchen by my wrist and the next morning it was twice the size it should be because of the swelling. I came up with another excuse but when I went round to visit a friend, Eleanor, I told her my Dad had done it and that I couldn't take any more. What I didn't know was that her Mum had been listening through the door. She called social services and they visited the house. The result? Another performance from Mum, another accusation that I was a liar and this time I was told that I could no longer spend time with Eleanor.

I was failing at school. Years later, I spoke with a teacher and asked her what she remembered about me. She said that I seemed like a little girl – lost – and desperate to please her friends. I suppose that explains why I'd spend so much time clowning around at the back of the class. But she also pointed out something else that I had never thought of, but know to be true: she said that you can't teach an unhappy or angry child. I had arrived at school on the 'at risk' register but then at my school, it wasn't that uncommon. It was difficult for my teachers as although they were aware that I was unhappy at home, no one was allowed to ask me directly. So I spent much of my time messing about, mostly with Helen. I'd sit at the back, swinging on my chair and chatting, even falling right off sometimes, but if this bothered my teachers, it never bothered me. Letters would be sent home but the daft thing was, they'd arrive at my friend Helen's house the day before mine. She'd let me know in school and I'd just delay leaving until the post had come, find the letter and dump it.

I was 13 years old, I didn't look it and I acted younger than my years, too. I think that's why it must have been a shock for a neighbour, who was also a Jehovah's Witness and a church friend of Mum's, when, one morning, she saw me pass and drop something. I stood in my neatly ironed school uniform and said, 'Oh fuck it!' I didn't see her, but I heard all about it when I got home from school. Dad made me pay the consequence and so I made sure that I never walked that street to school but walked through the park, so I could say, 'Oh fuck it,' without worrying about busybodies. To me, it seemed that people would worry and act on my bad language but about very little else that was bad in my life concerned them.

In truth, I wasn't that angry with the neighbour. To me, the source of all my pain was the man my mother called her husband. Despite not celebrating birthdays or Christmas, the great irony was that we were expected to celebrate their anniversary. This was the time of year when the children got presents. When I was about 8, their anniversary turned into one of the happiest days of my life as I had been given the thing I'd most wanted in the world: a pair of roller blades. I never took them off – I even climbed a tree in them, falling out and breaking a wrist. I'd do handstands in them, roller blade everywhere and generally be a menace. They were so precious to me. Even now, I break into a grin just thinking about them. I had nagged Mum about them for ages and when she told me with a smile that I would be getting something very special the next day, I honestly couldn't think what it could be. She even said, 'I'll give you a clue – the letters R and B.' I was so used to being disappointed where toys were concerned that I spent the night thinking about food that began with 'R' and 'B', as I thought the best I could hope for was sweets. But it was the boots. They were blue with white laces and yellow wheels, with red and yellow detailing on the sides – I thought they were just perfect.

But by the time I reached 13, that happy memory was almost buried and their anniversary celebrations felt like a sick joke to me. It was the one time of year when they'd dress up and go out for a meal. We'd still get a gift each, but what ran through my mind was confusion about how she could celebrate the day, still want to stay with him and endure another year. I couldn't understand it. As part of my general troublemaking, I would sneak into their room and look through their things. I had found their stash of condoms and had blown some up, filled them with water and thrown them out of the bathroom window. Mum was horrified and asked what on earth I thought I was doing. 'Using those balloons,' I told her. Again, hoping that she would stand up to me but nothing came of it.

But then I made a far darker discovery. Hidden in the drawer of Dad's bedside cabinet was a knife. It fascinated me. Why was it there? It was no ordinary knife – it looked like a sort of hunting knife with a heavy handle. I would pick it up and once even dragged my finger over it. It was so sharp, it cut my finger with ease and I watched the blood rise and run down towards my wrist. Time and again I crept into their room, opened the drawer and took out the knife. Some nights, I would even take it into my room and sleep with it under my pillow. To this day, I don't know why. I do know that I thought about using it on Dad, thinking that the only way I'd survive would be to kill him. In the light of all that has happened, my memory of one night still makes me shiver. Dad was in bed asleep and I stole into the room. Mum was downstairs. I was holding the knife and I can remember the weight in my hand as I stood over him, watching him breathe steadily as he lay on his back. Then, he turned over. It was as if a spell had been broken.

Suddenly, I was terrified he would wake up. I left the room and it was the last time that I picked up the knife.

My fantasies about killing him now seemed impossible to fulfil but the rest of my life was starting to unravel. I desperately wanted Mum to leave but in my heart I knew she wouldn't. I'd fight with her, hating her for her weakness; I'd suffer at Dad's hands and school seemed increasingly pointless to me. I remember watching an episode of some soap or other and there was a girl diagnosed with a brain tumour. The next day, I went to school and told everyone I was ill and that I was dying, that I had a brain tumour.

The attention, the sympathy, felt right for a while. But if I was in pain, few really knew why and those who did never helped stop it. It would be just as well if I did have a brain tumour I thought, then everyone would realise what pain I was in, and in the end, I could lay down like my grandfather had, and Dad would have to watch over me and tell everyone, 'No, she's not coming back this time.'

But it was not to be my own but another whose death gave me a glimpse of freedom. A call had come from Italy: Nonna was seriously ill and not expected to live. Dad was clearly upset and made plans to visit his family to be with his mother at the end. After he left, there was the most incredible change at home. It was as if we had begun to breathe for the first time. Rather than fight Mum, I couldn't do enough for her. I helped out with cooking and other chores, and we'd talk and laugh together. Dad was to be gone for at least four weeks as he had to arrange the funeral and sort out Nonna's finances. So Mum arranged for the rest of us to go to Butlins. We had a simply brilliant time without him. Dad had written to Mum to let her know how long he expected to be away and she had replied with her bombshell: she wrote to say that she didn't want him to come home. Everything had changed in Dad's absence: none of us were living in fear, and Mum had a glimpse of how straightforward life could be when she wasn't looking over for her shoulder or fretting about her husband's next outburst. I was a different child, too. I remember her telling me she had put in a letter: 'Even Natalia is doing as she's told now that you are not here. She is as good as gold.' I don't know what Dad's reaction was, and frankly, I didn't care. All I cared about was that he might be gone for good. It was a euphoric atmosphere at home: we were all light-headed with the idea that we had got rid of him, but part of this was driven by the realisation that it couldn't last, that it couldn't be that simple, that he'd be back.

What arrived first was a video. It was extraordinary. Dad had taped a message to Mum, pleading with her to be allowed back home. He railed on about the oath that she had made to God, but the most direct threat concerned himself. It was simple: take me back or I'll kill myself. My death will be on your hands for eternity. It rocked Mum and simply destroyed her faith in the decision she had made. She was ashen and sat down with us to ask what we thought. 'Good, let him!' I said. But even then, I knew the game was over; that once again, he'd won. Back he came, and back we went into the awful knowledge that soon we'd break his laws and have to pay the price.

The one outlet I had at school, the one lesson I truly enjoyed, as I've already said, was Drama with Mrs Hunt, the one teacher I truly trusted. She was just lovely – she really cared about her pupils, not just their achievements in the classroom. Mrs Hunt must have spotted a mile off that I was troubled and she always made the effort to chat with me and ask how things were. This was the first adult I felt I could trust and I confided in her that my home life was a mess, but that I was deeply ashamed of it and could talk to no one but her. She listened and encouraged me to talk to a child therapist again, telling me that it could be arranged so that I would see the therapist on my own, not with the rest of the family. I thought it would be good to be able to talk to an outsider but I soon ran up against a brick wall: I was asked what would I like to do about the situation at home. It was made clear that if I wanted professional intervention, it would mean the risk of foster care and there was no guarantee that Daniel and I would stay together. All I wanted was for them to remove Dad and leave us all at home together, but what was suggested was very different from what I dreamed of. The idea that I could be parted from Daniel and Mum filled me with horror. It sounded as if Mum's warnings were right and so I stopped the sessions. Once or twice I said I'd go back, but the idea that I could be responsible for splitting up the family was too much to cope with.

But Mrs Hunt understood and she stuck by me. Over the next couple of years she proved vital to my sanity, too. In her class, I felt as if I could just forget about everything for a while, but I had the safety net of talking to her if it all became too much. She also intervened in the strangest of ways, helping to keep me from driving Mum crazy. I had nagged and nagged her for a pair of shoes with a sort of zig-zag pattern underneath. They were fairly expensive and Mum had resisted for a while, but in the end, she gave in. I wore them for the first time and due to my trek through the park, found that the soles filled with mud, and I hated that. So I blithely told Mum that I would never wear them again. She was distraught. Money was still an issue but more than that, my bloody-mindedness would get back to Dad and I would receive another hiding. I didn't care and made sure she felt awful by being really childish, clearly unwilling to see her point of view. Her point of view didn't matter — it never did in the house so why should it matter to me now? In desperation, she turned to Mrs Hunt. My teacher called us both in, and in front of Mum, she made me see sense. She made me promise to wear them for that term at least and it was the perfect compromise. I saw reason because Mrs Hunt gave me a way out without backing down, something I was finding it harder and harder to do even though I could see it made the people around me, who really cared for me, suffer.

With Mrs Hunt's encouragement, I grew to enjoy Drama all the more. I loved her lessons, and it was because of her that I threw myself into getting parts in plays such as *Oliver Twist* and *The Little Shop of Horrors*. Mum would come along, and she always said sweet things to me and encouraged me. I can remember Dad coming along once but he said very little. He wasn't one to give 'false praise', though he was always happy to point out his children's shortcomings. But this desire to point out where we were going wrong and how much better he could do took a twist I never expected when Mrs Hunt sent a note home about a drama festival. Rather than just perform, we could write, or get someone we knew to write a piece as well. Dad took up the challenge, telling me he would write something worthy of performing.

It was a disaster: he penned a piece about the slaughter of the innocents in Iraq. The first Gulf War had filled the TV screens and newspaper columns with awful stories about innocent civilians who suffered and lost their lives but a school festival wasn't exactly the right place to air those concerns, and certainly not through a dramatic monologue. To give you an idea, one of my friends acted out 'I must, I must, I must improve my bust' to huge laughter and applause. I had to follow with a disturbing account of children in Baghdad dying. The silence afterwards was only slowly broken by polite applause and I was deeply, horribly embarrassed. The extraordinary thing was that when the judges gave their verdict, I came second. I think this was in part to save my blushes, and I felt so relieved. I came out after the presentation had ended and Mum beamed at me. Dad, however, said that I would never be an actress, that I just wasn't good enough and if I had any talent at all, I would have come first, thanks to his piece. I was stunned into silence. Pretty uncharacteristic for me but I vowed not to involve Dad ever again. I was never good enough for him.

But I wasn't the only one suffering. I have often wondered why Dad wasn't violent towards Mum but as the years have passed, I've come to realise that he didn't use his fists because he didn't have to. It was clear, he told her many times, that if she did not obey him, he would take her life or his own, and that he would find a way to make sure she never saw her children again. Allied with that was his campaign to knock her down, to tell her she was worthless, and then to build her up, telling her she was beautiful in his eyes. It was macabre. He was her jailer, but also her one hope of freedom – for if it was not by serving him, she'd be damned for an eternity. By obeying him, deliverance could be hers. He would swing from terror to a caress and I think now that Mum knew in her heart of hearts that she would never, ever be free. All she could do was try and limit the damage he caused us, and somehow keep us together as a family.

But I no longer trusted her judgement or her ability ever to stand up to him. I was alone: Daiana had gone, Emmanuele had found a YTS scheme and was out of the picture, and Daniel was still a young boy. I had left school with poor qualifications. The only thing I'd excelled in was Drama and so I managed to get a place on a Performing Arts course at a further education college. To earn a bit of money, I'd got a job in McDonalds. Then, one day, my friend introduced me to David. He was five years older than me, a student at Nottingham University, and he became my ticket out of Scunthorpe and the start of a new life – at least, that's what I believed. What I didn't know them was that I was setting in play the endgame of my life with Mum and Dad, and that two years later, my mother would be dead.

CHAPTER FIVE

RUNNING AWAY

Even now, looking back and dragging up memories, I'm aware of how much I've missed and how much I've buried. Sometimes, it feels like I'm locked into a cat-and-mouse game with my mind, catching glimpses and moments from an event, but often as I try to focus, I feel shut out.

Not all of it's bad; it's not all horror. Recently, I found an old photograph. I don't know who took it: could it have been Dad? I was standing in the playground of my primary school holding Mum's hand and I'm wearing a butterfly costume that she made. I'm beaming at the camera, and behind me there's a mural painted on the wall, filled with lovely bright images, including a butterfly just like me. I was overwhelmed when I saw it. Memories of the play yard, and how proud I was of the costume Mum had made, all came flooding back. She was so clever. I've since returned to the school but the mural has gone: it's just a blank wall now. If it wasn't for the photograph, that day in my life would have been whitewashed too. It's incredible how you can be pitched back to how you felt over twenty years ago – I was so small and excited, holding Mum's hand. All from the chance discovery of one photograph.

Some deeply buried memories aren't so easy to deal with, though. I caught up with an old friend not too long ago and she told me that, growing up, if I wasn't at home, she'd know where to find me. The two of us had built a den, not too far away from my dad's allotment, but hidden, secret and somewhere I'd feel safe. I would spend hours there, telling my friend Eleanor that this time I'd run away for good, and she'd leave me there, or find me there, depending on what had erupted at home. Eleanor remembers something I can't, how she found me in the den one day, crying, and I lifted up my T-shirt to show her how bruised I was. I don't remember. There are times when I am too exhausted, too ashamed and too empty to step back into the past.

But some things are easy to recall and still make me smile, like how appealing the idea of running away was. I do remember announcing that I was planning to leave and that my plan was a simple one: I was in love with Howard from Take That and I was on my way to London to meet him, and then move in and live with him for good. Oddly, the idea of running away with Howard was based on more than just falling for a picture of him in a magazine. Take That had been to our school; it was their early days of promotion, part of manager Nigel Martin-Smith's master plan to build a fan base of avid girl teens, and I was lucky enough to have met them. It turned out to be a pretty bizarre episode in my teenage life. I was 14 and had already heard of Take That, but they weren't the huge band they were destined to become. Nevertheless, I thought they were great and had to try and devise a way to meet them.

Along with a classmate, we approached the headmaster and suggested that we interview them after the show and then either write up the interview as an extra piece of English homework or use it as the start of a new school newspaper, as the school didn't have one. I presented it all as an opportunity as I was sure that this would be the start of my life as a music journalist. This was nonsense but I'd said enough to convince the head and he agreed. Perhaps he was just amazed that I was volunteering to do more English coursework, I'm not sure, but the important thing was that after the show they put on in the school hall, which was great, my friend and I could make a meal out of saying: 'Actually, we've got access to go backstage and meet the band.' It was without doubt, one of the very few moments of triumph I enjoyed at school.

We went 'backstage' and we were both giggling with nerves and excitement. The five boys were fantastic – just incredibly professional, enthusiastic and friendly. But at the time, I didn't think that was part of their professionalism, didn't understand how important word-of-mouth advertising was to a new band. I really thought it was because they liked me. Howard in particular, was lovely. He gave me a big hug and was really keen to talk. I had already made up my mind not to bother too much with Gary, and my friend had made it clear that Mark was hers, so that just left Howard, Jason and Robbie. Robbie was clearly the clown, really quite hyper. I had taken along a banner that I'd made from an old bed sheet and I'd painted 'Take That – We Love You' on it. At one point, Robbie started fooling around with it and we ended up wrestling to the floor, with Robbie pretending to strangle me with the banner. As I said, the whole thing was bizarre, but it remains a really happy memory in what were often pretty grim teenage years.

The result was that within twenty minutes, I was madly in love with Howard and told him so. He said, 'Aah, that's nice. I love you too.' My friend and I then declared our love for them all. Robbie said, 'We're playing in Hull tonight. Why don't you come along?' We promised we would. At this point, I think we'd done very little of the 'interview'. I can't really remember writing anything down, but the whole thing was shot on video by another pupil. I never saw the tape and I think it was stolen. I didn't care about that – I just wanted to get to Hull that night, but of course, it was out of the question. There was only one occasion when I got to stay out 'late' at a disco. It was organised by the school, no alcohol was allowed and the event was finished by 10pm, but I was only allowed to join my friends if my dad cycled along behind me on the way there and on the way back! It was entirely humiliating and the only way I could cope was to ignore him entirely. It must have looked really funny – an earnest, balding Italian cycling at walking pace behind a 15-year-old, obviously determined to ignore him. But I didn't see the funny side at all –it just made me want to scream and find a way to escape for good. So the idea of running away appealed and I remembered that

Howard had said that the band were about to move to London. So that was that: I would run away to London to be with him.

It's strange to think of it now, but I had little idea that my running away adventure would soon play out for real; that only a couple of years after taking down my Take That posters, I'd be homeless and trying to scrape my life together in a hostel for battered women. But I can honestly tell you that there are far worse things waiting for you in life on the streets than not having a home to call your own. There's more violence and degradation hidden from you on your walk into work than you can ever imagine. Perhaps you look away – it's hard not to, and it's something I've done myself as I pass people in doorways. We may share the same streets but compared to the steady existence most of us enjoy, it's a life lived with no boundaries and little hope. The first thing you discover is that you're worth nothing. And you'll find it hard to avoid violence handed out casually by strangers, just waiting for the chance to find a young woman stupid enough to think she's seen it all. But for now, that was all ahead of me, unknown and just another part of the journey that had begun before I was even born – parcelled up as another trial to endure before I could even begin to make sense of my short life.

Back when I met David, I thought that I had already reached an end to my nightmares. Here was a man who was so different from my dad it took my breath away. He was so kind and gentle, and in all the time I knew him, he never raised his voice or told me what I could or couldn't do.

Here was a man who not only seemed to like me but promised a way out of Scunthorpe; who told me he loved me and that he wanted to look after me.

David was at university and was working his year out from Nottingham as part of his business degree. He was due to go back to Mansfield, where he was working, within a few weeks and he asked me to go with him. I was working at McDonalds, but it was just a job to tide me over while I did my Performance Arts course and the idea came to me that I could transfer my job to Mansfield and that would be that. It might sound odd that I didn't think about staying to complete my course, but David was offering me the chance of total escape and frankly, no academic qualification could compete with that.

Part-thrilled, part-terrified. I told Daiana my plan and she urged me to be careful. She said that Dad would never stand for it, that he'd probably kill me just for thinking about it. My mum's view was similar, telling me to forget it and saying that even suggesting it to Dad would probably lead him to locking me in my room indefinitely. But I saw David as my one opportunity to get away from Dad and so I went to the police. I asked them for advice and whether, at 17, Bruno could simply say no and imprison me. They said that he couldn't, and that as David was in employment and able to finance our life, and as we had accommodation arranged, there was nothing my dad could do: I was free to go.

I had talked to David about Dad. He listened to me and said how sorry he was but the gulf between us as a couple was already there, no matter how I tried to pretend that it wasn't. He had no true idea of what I'd lived with and how the scars of it were impacting on my behaviour towards him. As much as he cared for me, I couldn't truly trust him. His easy-going nature left me wary. I felt that even though he knew all Dad had done, it was so remote from his experience that it was, to him, just a bit of a sad story about my past. It's hard enough for anyone who has not been through the same experience to understand how growing up with brutality can cauterise your emotions long after the events themselves have passed. Yet even though this was my life, it was impossible for me to see how my past had laid the seed of destruction that would shatter the hopes I had for my future.

Back then, all I could focus on was the escape. I secretly transferred my job and planned when I'd speak to Dad. But it was Mum's turn first. She was reduced to tears and begged me not to say anything and not to leave; I was abandoning her. She even said, 'Don't leave, you are the only girl left – please don't leave me.' I was harsh and told her that I didn't care, that I wasn't concerned that she'd be alone with him and I stated coldly that I had nothing to stay for. I remember her tears and that I walked away afterwards. When the day came to tell my dad I was amazed how calm I was – but this was only the start of the day's astonishments. I told him about David, what a good student he was, what great prospects he had, how we had a job and a flat and then I made it very clear that I had told the police everything. The police knew about our conversation too and my fears about his reaction. He was silent and then he said, 'Well, I don't agree with what you are doing and let me make it clear that you are not leaving with my blessing, but I love you, and your mother and I are here for you.'

I will never forget watching Mum's face – her jaw nearly hit her chest. She was pale and she couldn't believe what she had heard. I think we were both taken aback but Dad remained placid. It was the most extraordinary thing. I think Mum understood what my motivations were where David was concerned. I can remember coming home after that first time David and I had sex. I was 17 and had finally lost my virginity, about three years later than most of friends. I asked, 'So what's all the fuss about, Mum?' I don't think she knew what to do – she was taking in the horror of the fact that I had had sex (after all, this was the house that had banned Tampax), and also the fact that I was so blithe and confused as to what it was supposed to mean. I was underwhelmed as I imagined the pact I had sealed with David would mean so much more to me. What was so evidently missing, at least to Mum's shrewd gaze, was in my feeling towards David. I simply didn't love him. I should have – he was a good and caring man – but at that point, being in love was beyond me. Agreeing to have sex was just my part of the bargain, I thought.

Mum was shocked and tried to say something along the lines of, 'You'll know when sex is right when you are with the right person.' But, once again, I shot her down in flames, saying, 'And what would *you* know about that? You've only ever been with Dad.' She bit her lip and, as ever, concentrated on giving me best counsel, and I let it wash over me. Whatever she thought or felt mattered less to me than the knowledge that I was off to Mansfield and that I would finally start to live my life.

Despite Mum's tears, I was so happy to be leaving that

day. I set off in David's car with just a few boxes and a suitcase, and I enjoyed every minute of the drive south. It took less than an hour, and a half but it felt like a light year to me. The strange thing was that once we'd moved in, all I could think about was setting up house like a fifties housewife. I was only 17, but I was acting the only role I'd ever known for a woman in the home. I was behaving like my mother. I'd cook basic dishes because I never learned to cook properly as Daiana had, and I'd clean and fuss over the flat, never thinking that David and I should be going out and partying. We'd stay at home and watch TV, spend a huge amount of time in supermarkets planning our meals and generally carrying on like a couple who'd been together for 25 years, not a few months. On Sundays, David would pop out to the bookies and I'd prepare a traditional roast, just as Dad would have expected.

Not that I was unhappy – I just didn't know how else to behave or what was expected of me. David was as easygoing as ever and happy to have his domestic arrangements run so smoothly. He wasn't selfish – he'd help tidy up, he'd cook the occasional meal and help with the washing up – but I don't know why he didn't wonder why we were living as we were. He was sensitive, he'd always try to understand where I was coming from even though I never really opened up to him, and perhaps that held him back. His idea of a good time had been to sit in pubs and have a few pints, but it wasn't mine. I don't really know why, but this would put me on edge. Perhaps I worried that if he got drunk he'd change and somehow act out the violence I thought all men were capable of. I didn't really drink. When I was 14, a friend gave me some alcopop or other and it made me throw up violently. I didn't trust drink and had never touched drugs; it just didn't feel comfortable with the lack of control I saw in friends around me. It scared me.

So David would just have one or two pints and we'd come away, and slowly, the number of people we'd see fell away. We were a self-sufficient unit of two, padding around the shops when most teens were at festivals and getting ripped. Never mind, I thought, this is how I like my life and I'm even free to go out to work. I don't know what David made of it when I asked his permission to carry on working. I do remember he said in a patient and slightly baffled way, 'Yes, of course, Natalia – you do what you want to do.' And I thought, wow, isn't that cool? I've got away with that! I didn't know it then but the years of being guarded and feeling that I had to hide what I was thinking had taken their toll. David never really stood a chance despite my best efforts to go through the motions, and the ultimate pantomime proved to be a visit from my parents. I cooked a three-course meal and we all sat through lunch acting out the roles expected of us. Bruno and Elva were dressed smartly and Dad was jovial and at his talkative best. They murmured their approval to everything we'd done to the flat and we all sat smiling. Yet in the back of my head, I was thinking, If Dad gets up now and walks over and hits me, David won't stop him. He might walk out with me but he wouldn't stop him.

Of course, Dad did nothing of the sort. They just headed back to Scunthorpe with cheery goodbyes. What Mum really made of it, I'll never know. She was probably happy that Dad had come to some sort of acceptance as he very much approved of David's chosen career and determination to make it in the business world – and, after all, Mum had been the same age as me when they met. While Dad's relative calm would have helped, my phone calls would not.

Only two days after arriving in Mansfield, I called Mum. I was in tears saying, 'Mum, I really miss you. I really do and I love you. Tell me you love me.' This from the daughter who told her she hated her, who'd stolen from her, who told her for years that she wished her husband dead. Now I was on the phone begging her to tell me that she loved me.

'Of course I do,' was all she'd say.

'No, tell me you love me, let me here you say it,' I pleaded.

But she never did. She kept her emotions tightly in check.

Eventually, Dad came to the phone. 'Natalia, your mother and I love you. You know we do.'

But it wasn't from him I wanted to hear it. Why wouldn't she tell me?

In all their years together, I never heard Mum tell Dad that she loved him. He would tell her, loudly and demonstrably, as part of his 'caressing', but she would stay tight-lipped. Now her unruly daughter was making the same declarations, and asking that she say out loud what she wanted to hear. Was I acting too much like my father, pushing her one way and then pulling her another? That wasn't how it felt. I felt so alone and I needed Mum more than ever. I truly loved her and felt sorry for the pain I had put her through. But was it too late? Had I pushed her too far away? It was too painful for me to even think about, and so I'd call her; sometimes, ten times a day.

'Natalia,' Mum would say, 'you spoke to me only half an hour ago. What is it?'

'Mum, I just want to know what you're doing,' I'd reply. 'Tell me what you are doing. I miss you.'

I told Mum I loved her far more than I ever told David. He was hard at work studying and he never probed too much into my state of mind or emotions. We just carried on and every day I went to my job at McDonalds. I've no idea how long we would have drifted on in this way, but work suddenly became a problem. The manager of the store was a nice guy called Simon and we got on fairly well. I was about a year into the job when I realised that his friendly chats were fast turning into open flirtation. This threw me and I'd say time and again, 'I have a boyfriend and we live together.' Far from putting Simon off, he just became more insistent that he liked me and wanted to be with me.

Sometimes, he'd walk the same route home with me, just chatting and sharing jokes about work. I know that I could have frozen him out and told him to get lost, but there was some part of me that couldn't. I did like him, I felt a kind of buzz around him that I didn't when I was with David, and I let him tell me things about how pretty I was, and other stuff that men say, because it was good to hear. I never felt I was all the things he said about me and so when he asked yet again if I'd go for a drink, I hesitated. He said, 'Oh come on, Natalia, everyone from work is going to be there.' So I agreed. The pub was called the Woolpack and I didn't know where it was, but Simon said not to worry, that he'd walk me there. When we arrived, no one from work was there. That's when he told me that he'd planned it this way and begged me to stay for just one drink. I felt awkward, but agreed and then set off to walk home. Simon walked with me and we were about halfway to my house when he stopped me and kissed me. I could pretend that I was horrified but I wasn't. I enjoyed it and then came the horror. What have I done? I thought.

I pushed Simon off and marched home, mortified that I'd betrayed David. When he came home, I told him everything and said how sorry I was. David was upset but not angry, and didn't even blame me. I said, 'I have to go now, I have been unfaithful and we have to split up.' But David thought this was an over-reaction and told me not to be silly, to calm down and to sleep on it. He felt it would all be OK by the morning and that maybe I could work in another branch if Simon made me uncomfortable. He said not to worry, that he had taken advantage of me and it was only a kiss after all. But I was adamant: I had behaved like a fallen woman and would have to pay the price by leaving. I must have seemed unbalanced to him, but in the back of my mind was my dad's voice. I had sinned and would suffer.

It was Dad's voice that also made me believe that now that I had let Simon kiss me, I must end my relationship with David and settle for Simon. So I picked up my things and called Simon. Amazingly, he said fine and we moved in together. The whole thing seems bizarre now, but I told Simon that I wanted to go back to Scunthorpe as I as keen to be near Mum. He agreed to get a transfer and, in a strange twist, we moved in with my sister and her husband as Daiana had a senior role at McDonalds, not based in a restaurant but an office, and said she'd help.

I think I was sleepwalking my way through this part of my life, half-demanding the things I wanted, like moving to be closer to Mum, and half-drifting into a relationship with Simon as I couldn't think of a way out of it. But I didn't stay at my sister's very long. I took a serious dislike to her husband and told Simon to carry on renting from them and that I would move out. I guess it was a way of breaking up by degrees as I didn't have the courage to say that I had made a mistake, but then fate helped out when I saw a job advertised at a holiday camp in Cleethorpes. I applied without ever imagining that I'd get the job, but somehow I did, and soon moved an even smaller amount of my stuff into a static caravan, sharing with two other holiday-camp staff.

I can hardly believe that three of us shared a caravan, two girls and one lad who was running the football sessions for the children. My job was to help organise activities and games, and it soon became clear to Simon that I had no interest in resuming my relationship with him. In fact, I didn't want to resume my relationship with anyone as the camp was a sealed-off environment where most of the workers were intent on having a wild time. As soon as we were off-duty, we'd party. I still wasn't a drinker but it was the first time I'd been introduced to smoking dope. Part of me was so determined to shake off the mistakes I thought I'd made that the giggly effects of smoking, and staying up and messing around, were exactly what I was looking for. I had a blast and felt like a teenager for the first time. Everyone wanted the same escape and I thought I'd go on like this indefinitely – until I got caught on camera, kissing another member of staff: a DJ. We were hauled into the head office the next day and asked to explain our actions. You could stay up all night partying but the absolute rule was that camp workers were not to have affairs with each other. It seemed ridiculous and there was nothing to explain: we were caught snogging, in black and white. So we were fired. I had only been working there for two months but the idea of having to leave panicked me. Mum had said come home, but I had refused as I was still too scared of Dad. 'I won't come home,' I told her. 'He'll be waiting and he'll just hit me again.'

I was out of a job and with no place to live. Simon was still renting from my sister so I felt I couldn't go there. There were two families that I had got on really well with at the holiday camp and during the course of the day I told them both what had happened. Both were kind and sympathetic and said I could come and stay with them: one family was from Doncaster, the other from Leicester. It seems incredible to me now but I chose to put my life into the hands of strangers rather than risk going back home. I felt I was a failure because I had lost David through my own immorality and I couldn't imagine surviving back in Dad's house, so once I'd packed my things, I headed to Doncaster.

The family from Doncaster were a single mum and her younger daughter. They were very kind and allowed me to live in their spare room for a month or so. I could have got a job in a McDonalds, I suppose but without really being aware of it, I was heading for a fall. I had no real interest in living in Doncaster; I was there merely because I could not think of what else to do. Mum would call and ask time and again for me to come home saying, 'Natalia, I don't like to think that you are living with strangers.' But I refused. She was right, of course. I *was* with strangers, and no matter what their good intentions were, I had no ties to them and I was ultimately beyond their help. I knew I was drifting; it was almost as if I was waiting for something to break my fall but nothing came and I felt that I had outstayed my welcome.

This is the point where I could have gone home, my tail between my legs. Instead, I called the family in Leicester and asked if their offer still stood. They said yes, and so I set off to stay with them. The situation at their house was far more complicated. The eldest son, Jamie, was keen for us to get involved and I saw no real reason not to. Little else was going on in my life so it was an easy distraction as we spent our time looking for work and messing around. The problem was that the youngest son, Lee, had taken a shine to me, too, and would often make advances when his brother's back was turned. In truth, I felt very little for either of them and was horrified when a fight broke out between them.

Their mum quite rightly sensed that the root of the household's trouble was me. I wasn't sure what I was doing or not doing, just my being there was enough to disrupt everything, it seemed. Any charitable feelings she may have had on holiday disappeared when the practicalities of housing an unhappy and directionless 18-year-old girl, an object of competition between her sons, came to light. She told me to leave, to get out and I didn't want a scene. The odd thing is, no matter how much I'd battled with Dad and no matter how used I was to being shouted at, I can't bear confrontation. I'll do nearly everything I can to avoid it – it makes me feel genuinely ill. If you were to stand up and yell at me now, I'd be the one who backed down and walked off; I wouldn't even meet your eye.

I left the house without knowing where to turn. In my heart, I still couldn't bring myself to go home and ask for forgiveness. It was all I could do to keep trudging onwards without having to think about the scene that I would have to play out with Dad. So I walked to the nearest park and simply sat down on a bench. I didn't really realise at this point that I was sitting where I'd be forced to sleep. I suppose I was numbed by what was going on, and besides, Jamie had decided to storm out of his house and had told me that if I had to leave then he would too. It was a ludicrous situation. I was facing a night on a park bench, but I hung onto the fact that I wasn't alone, as that would have terrified me, and at least it was summer so the temperature wouldn't drop too low. We spent a couple of nights in the park. After the first night, we realised this was far from a game and fear about where I could turn started to set in. When we saw Lee walking into the park, I feared the worst – in fact, he'd come to give us some food and a bit of money. I think he felt guilty and as bewildered as we did. In the daytime, Jamie and I visited an advice centre and our options were laid out. There was no temporary accommodation for Jamie, but if I was on my own, a bed would be allocated to me at the battered wives' shelter.

It was clear enough: I would be better on my own. I sent Jamie home and waited to be collected to go to the shelter. Once you are in the hands of social services, you feel only in part reassured. You feel humiliation at having to explain your story and a reluctance to engage with even the most sympathetic case worker. I was having trouble dealing with the way my life was unravelling and the most I could do was mimic my Mum by quietly nodding along with whatever I felt they needed to hear. I was shut off from everyone and just wanted to rest.

The shelter was an eye-opener. It was desperate. Somehow the cheap furniture, murals and children's wallpaper made me feel all the more depressed. There were women and children there with stories more harrowing than mine and yet within minutes, I recognised the hurt and cover-up in the eyes and actions of many. Some were addicted to pills, others alcohol, still more too depressed to even begin to deal with the demands of their children. These were women just a few years older than me in some cases, who'd had their lives crushed by violence and degradation and yet they were trying to create a life for their children to shield them from further damage. Some were my mum's age.

I thought of Mum and it made me realise that even if she'd run away from Dad, her suffering wouldn't have ended. It's a tough and long struggle to wean yourself from an abusive relationship, that frightening circle of love, need and ruin. Like the frog in a cooking pot that doesn't jump out if the heat is only turned up gradually, many woman don't make it and they stay with their abusive partners year in year out, losing their spirit and dignity, and their children by degrees. Some try to leave but fail and go back into their partners' arms, just not able to find the strength to pick up the pieces of their lives and start again.

If you are a mother, God help you. You've no money, no home, and children who are confused and angry, who and ask so much from you when you feel hollowed out. Thankfully, some women do make it, and as I was told, they were the ones who found strength for their children, a strength they often didn't have for themselves. They are the unrecognised and true heroes – women who re-start their lives with less than nothing, so their kids don't have to live in fear anymore.

I'd listen to their stories and then go back to my room, which had a single bed and a cabinet for my things. And I thanked God that I only had myself to look after. I saw some of the kids smoking pot and thanked God again that I only had myself to mess up with my casual use of drugs. Pot was part of my life now. It was easy to find, and smokers were usually happy to have someone to smoke with: it eases the time even more and you feel like you are all in it together. You understand each other even if everyone on the outside can't; you ask few questions of yourself and even less of each other.

I'd smoke mostly over the road, in a park, with a girl from the hostel. She, along with others, taught me a few dodges: how to sign on, as that way, you only had to pay £5 a week rent. If I was working, it would be £100. My plan was to try and get shifts at McDonalds but it wasn't going to be easy as you had to sign in and out of the shelter and the hours were restricted from 10am to 5pm.

Signing in was essential as the staff had to monitor where everyone was and make sure that no men wandered in. This last point was vital as quite a few of the women lived in fear of their lives. Most had been assaulted and I was told a scary statistic: of the hundred or more who die every year at the hands of their partners, more than half are killed once they have left. The most dangerous time for women in violent relationships can be the time after she walks out: this is the 'breaking point' for many men. But it isn't just women who are at risk; every woman in that shelter feared for her children.

At least one child a week is murdered by a parent. And the bleakest scenario of all is that of the fathers who track down their ex-partners, gain access to their children and deliberately set out to kill them, leaving the mother alive. There's a chilling and twisted logic to the act, for it's a far greater a punishment than taking her life – women left with the unending pain of knowing she will never see her children again. It's the ultimate punishment carried out by a man who would have fathered her children and told her that no one loved her quite as he does. A few years ago, I read about the case of a woman called Samantha. Her ex killed their four little boys by gassing them in his car but first he made sure that they called their mother, Samantha, as they died, to tell her they loved her. It was years since I had left the shelter but that story threw me back into that feeling of desperation and incomprehension. Is it any wonder that many women depressed from a life of violence seek an easy few minutes' relief from smoking or drinking? I would never condemn those who do, but I do know that smoking added to my troubles; it didn't relieve them.

I had managed to get a few shifts at McDonalds and so I had a little cash. The girl I had befriended, Leanne, was happy to let me tag along to her drinking and smoking sessions down by the canal. Most evenings, there would be different faces there, but usually a core of familiar ones – men around my age and older, looking for the chance to waste a few hours and fool around. David had been to visit me a few days previously. He'd found out from Mum where I was and had driven down to check that I was OK. I signed him in, and he had looked around the shelter, but I was shocked to see his expression when he turned and asked me, 'Natalia, what are you doing here?' Here was this kind man, who still cared about me, but I couldn't deal with his concern and had refused his offer to take me home. That was in my mind, and I didn't want it to be, so the excuse to get wasted with Leanne seemed like a good one. I remember it was a warm sunny day, and I wore a black vest top that was too small for me and I was conscious that it made my boobs bulge more than I'd like but I had very little else to wear. I was also wearing a skirt, which I hardly ever do. I only had one skirt but it was too hot for my jeans.

When we reached the canal, there were about six lads and another two girls. I didn't recognise the girls. I recognised one of the guys; he had been there with us before and I got on with him really well. I don't recall his name, but I will call him Paul. I do remember he had a son that he hardly saw, and this was something we had previously talked about; something he found hard to deal with. Well, we were all drinking and smoking, and having a good time and for the time being I forgot that I was a homeless girl – the drink and smoke took all my pain and worry away.

Leanne came and told me she was wandering off with one

of the guys and asked if I was OK with that. I said I was because Paul was there and that he had said he would stay with me. I felt safe with him. After a while Paul was very stoned, and one of the guys who I had never met came and talked to us. After a while I knew he was chatting me up. When he went to get another drink, I asked Paul if this guy was OK and he said that although he didn't know him too well, he was a friend of a friend so he was sure he was alright.

He then said that I should, 'go for it'. So when the guy came back he asked if I wanted to go for a walk and I said sure. We walked for a short while, about two minutes, but I could see everyone behind us. We sat under a tree, with bushes beside us, we kissed and I thought that was fine. Then his hands started wandering up my top and I asked him to stop. That's when he said, 'Come on, you know you want it.' I tried to get up but he pulled me back towards him. I'm only 5ft 2in and he was much bigger than me. He started putting his hands up my skirt, and to my horror, he put his finger inside me and commented that I was wet, and said I must be enjoying it as women don't get wet if they're not enjoying it. I felt real fear and I said as calmly as I could that I didn't want him to carry on, but he pushed me down so I was on my back. Then he put his hand over my mouth and nose, and I found it hard to breathe.

He was propped up with his other hand and one of his knees on my chest, with the other pinning my leg. He carried on entering his fingers and then what felt like a fist inside me. All this time I still had my skirt and knickers on. He then told me he would take his hand away from my mouth if I promised to keep quiet. I nodded that I would.

As he took his hand away, I told him I couldn't breathe as he had it over my nose and he said sorry, and with his hand he pulled my knickers off. I asked him not to carry on and said that I wouldn't tell anyone, and that I would do whatever he wanted me to do to him but please, just not have sex with me. At this he smiled.

My mind was racing. I knew I couldn't break away from him and would do anything in the hope that he wouldn't hit me or hurt me any more. I weighed up that if I had to give him a blowjob, at least that meant I wouldn't be in pain. If I closed my eyes, I'm sure I could just pretend I was doing it to a boyfriend. He then undid his jeans – he took them off fully, just leaving his white socks on. I thought, thank God he's not going to hurt me. He then started kissing me and so I kissed him back, fearing that if I resisted, he'd get angry again. But it wasn't what interested him, because he then pinned me down, the same as before, with his hand over my mouth leaving just enough room for me to breathe. I tried to kick him and shove him off but to my horror, he hardly moved. He then inserted himself into me.

I remember the pain, I remember feeling that I should just stare at the clouds and try to make out shapes and think of something else until it was over. The strange thing was that he was going very slowly, as if he didn't want it to end. I just wanted him to come and get off me, but he was taking his time, as if he was making love to me, not raping me. Inside I was dying. My mind was split, half in disbelief, half by a desperate need to survive. I then heard a noise. I looked to my right and another guy from the group had arrived and saw what was going on.

The guy on top of me was saying, 'She's good she is, you want to have a go? As long as you keep your hand over her as she's a screamer.'

Whether this guy thought I was being raped or if I consented, I don't know but he said, 'Yes.'

'Well,' said the guy on top of me, 'hang about, let me finish her off and then you can have a go.'

At that the second man sat down, undid his trousers and stared masturbating. After what felt like a lifetime, but what was probably five minutes, the one on top of me came. He still had his hand on my mouth.

He kissed my cheek and said, 'It's OK — it will be over soon.'

The other guy got up and pulled down his trousers and I heard him say, 'Can you keep your hand on her mouth so I can keep mine free?'

After hearing the first guy agree, he said, 'I want her turned over.'

So they both turned me over.

I kicked and kicked, but felt my strength failing. They turned me over and the first guy sat with my face in his lap, with his hand over my mouth. The second guy then inserted himself into my bottom. God, I have never felt pain like it. I had never had anything there and it was more than I could bear. I moved my head up so I could see the guy with his hand over my mouth, and with tears falling down my face — stared at him, pleading with him for it to stop.

He just kissed my ear and said, 'It will be over before you know it and I bet you enjoyed it the first time rather than with this bloke.' Meanwhile, the second guy was thrusting as hard as he could, pulling my hair from behind.

He was grunting loudly and after what felt like forever, he finished and his body fell on top of me. I heard him get up and what sounded like him dressing. He then thanked the first guy and that was the last I ever saw of him. When the first guy let go of my mouth, I couldn't stop crying. I wanted to speak but I couldn't; I wanted to ask why.

He said, 'Sorry about that other bloke – I should of just left it at me. But don't even try and tell anyone; we'll just tell everyone that you were up for it. Besides, who's going to believe a homeless girl when we're both from good families? No one, that's who.'

Then he walked off.

I tried to pull myself together and got my knickers on. I noticed how much blood was all over the grass. It seemed more than a period. Somehow, I managed to get myself back to the hostel, crying all the way. I could hardly walk, my bottom was killing me. I got back to the hostel and ran a bath. It didn't stop the pain and there was blood in my bath. I wanted to ring my mum, but I kept thinking Dad will say, 'I told you so.' I was asking for trouble by choosing to wear a vest and skirt. Dad was right.

After about an hour in the bath I was still was numb with pain. Eventually, Leanne returned. Though I told her what happened, straightaway, I could see that she didn't want to hear. She tried to defend the men by saying, 'No, I think they are alright and perhaps they didn't mean it. Anyway, they told everyone about it and how you was loving it and how wet you was.'

I knew then that I was more alone than I had ever been in my life. I decided there and then never to tell anyone again. I phoned Mum. 'I want to come home,' I told her. Mum replied, 'Of course, we'll come in the morning.'

But it couldn't end there. I asked to speak to Dad. 'Promise me that you will never hit me again,' I asked.

The phone was silent for a second or so and then he said, 'I promise.'

It never even occurred to me to think about contacting the police. All I could feel was pain, a pain that I couldn't escape as it crawled through my mind, not just my body. Any idea I had of who I was or what I was had been destroyed in that one act. I was stupid, I'd deserved it. No matter how I tried, I knew that my life would never be the same again. I was going home, but home could not save me.

CHAPTER SIX

BACK HOME

So much time has passed since my days in the hostel and so many events have pushed me along, moving me further away from what happened that night. But it never leaves you, not really, to know something like that; it leaves a scar that never truly heals. It makes clear, in the starkest terms, that as a woman, you are always vulnerable. It destroys any trust you had, trust that you could look after yourself, trust in strangers. You learn that if a man is determined enough, he can do with you as he wishes and then walk off into the night, unscathed.

Is it possible to use another human being in that way and still believe that you are a good man? Sometimes I wonder if those men went on to get married, settle down and raise a family. I wonder if they have daughters and did they hold them in their arms and remember just what can happen to little girls. Do they try and protect them, knowing full well that the world is home to men willing to overpower a faceless girl and act out their sick whims? Can you be a father and look into your daughter's eyes and know that you were capable of rape? Perhaps they just block it out and carry on going to school plays and sports days, celebrating birthdays, the picture of a upstanding guy.

But my guess is, sometimes, they'll look at their daughters and be angry at how tough it is sometimes to forget. It wasn't someone else who used their knees to pin down the chest of a homeless 18-year-old, it was you. It wasn't someone else who had her held down as you anally raped her, it was you. Or did you carry on, finding other vulnerable girls, convincing yourself that they deserved it? But I'm sure that in the face of family and friends, you shake your head whenever you read another terrible story of a girl being attacked when it makes the news. Yet more than anyone else, you know that it's a bad, bad world out there – you just forgot to take your bow.

Most men never get caught. Most go back to their regular lives and regular jobs and regular homes. Most will write the whole thing off to some dirty slag who was asking for it. That was the thought that was left with me, alone on a bathroom floor crawling towards the bath. Dad was in my head again but this was a new fear I'd never known. All his warnings had come to pass. Mum and Dad arrived to collect me from the shelter in the morning. I hadn't slept but even though I could see fear and concern in Mum's eyes, she didn't press me to talk to her about what had happened and I was grateful for that. The shame was overwhelming. I felt I would fall apart at any moment, and that the surest thing that would push me over the edge would be for her to put her arms around me. She didn't, and we drove north to Scunthorpe in almost total silence. I pretended to sleep.

Seeing Daniel was the hardest. He was only 9 and so happy to see me. He ran over and tried to give me a huge hug, but I shrank away from him. It confused him and continued to do so over the next few weeks. Every time he approached, even though he was a young boy with that same bright smile, I felt myself recoil. He tried another tactic, talking to me about ice-skating, his new pastime. Daiana loved to skate; it was something we'd learned when we were younger and I still enjoy it now. When I get on the ice, I feel like I can fly. But it was different for Daiana and Daniel – they loved it with a passion, and Daiana found out that not only did Daniel enjoy it, but he had a natural talent, good enough to skate competitively. I was happy to hear him chat on excitedly about skating but I felt as if I was listening from a distance. Everything seemed clouded, and even ordinary conversation asked a lot of me.

Mum sensed something had happened but I was too wary to talk. I didn't want her to see that Dad had been right and I didn't want her to be disappointed in me. I decided to get some work as I was desperate not to dwell on the nightmare now haunting my waking hours as much as the dreams I had when I was asleep. I was desperate for company too, and could no longer bear to be alone. Once again, I got a job in McDonalds and tried to give my life routine but once I finished work, I would get wasted smoking with a group of people I knew. I wouldn't really call them friends, but that's how it often is with smokers – you smoke and that's enough. To me, at that time, it was the perfect drug. In those brief few hours, I liked myself and my life. I wasn't unhappy. It was like the promise of how life could be. Little did I realise that the quick chemical lie was laying the ground for deeper despair yet to be faced. I would work and party, but what was so much more damaging was that I would have sex with men I hardly knew.

I was a slag, and I never wanted to feel the way I had been made to feel that night ever again, and so I retaliated by acting first. I would have sex and despise the men who trotted after me. I had never enjoyed sex and this was the lowest point for me, just lying there almost motionless, waiting until it stopped. Yet none of the men who told me they 'cared' for me ever tried to understand why I was the way I was. I didn't care and I didn't want to care, and between drugs and chasing the next high, I thought I could keep outrunning my demons. My life at home had reached a sort of stalemate. Dad was careful to keep his distance from me and, in fact, never hit me again. Growing up, I had learned that if Mum said 'no', you could work on her and often her mind could be changed, but if Dad said 'no', that was it, it was set in stone. So even though he had undermined my whole childhood with his anger and control, I knew I could trust his word. He spoke to me to say that he would tell me if he disapproved of something I was doing, but he would not hit me. At this point, though, he never got a chance to give his views as the life I was leading outside the house was hidden from him.

Mum carried on as usual, the one steadying influence in

my life, but it was an uncharacteristic row that caused a new and unexpected crisis in the house. For some reason or another, she was planning a day out with Dad, and asked me to be around to take care of Daniel. I said that I couldn't because it was the same day as I'd planned to be out. Mum asked if I could change my plans and I explained that I couldn't as that was the first day free after pay day. If she could advance me the cash, I could go out earlier and make sure I was back to babysit Daniel on the day she wanted to go out. It all sounds trivial, the kind of mundane compromise that's thrashed out in a lot of households. But of course it was all done at volume because nearly every conversation in the Aggiano household was carried out at near-shouting levels. Emmanuele was upstairs and heard the commotion of me shouting back at Mum. Without warning, he came into the front room where I was sitting on the settee, and slapped me and thumped me around the head. It was a total shock. He'd just flipped because I was arguing with Mum. He thought a line had been crossed, even though he'd never challenged Dad over his behaviour towards Mum.

I freaked out. I could not bear being mistreated any more – just having him hit me made me feel everything that had happened wash over me again. Now, not even home was safe even though Dad had kept his word. Mum had come rushing in and pulled Emmanuele off me. She was horrified and furious with him. As soon as Dad came home she told him and even said Emmanuele should be thrown out. But I said no; I said that I would leave. I had been home for three months and now it seemed as if, once again, I had run out of options. I told Mum I would find a place to rent nearby and I think out of sheer guilt, Mum and Dad said they would help me by giving me the deposit I would need. It would take me a while to find a place but I would not stay there another night. I called Eleanor and she said that I could come and stay with her straightaway.

I packed what I had and set off, not realising that I would not be living at that address again with my mum alive. To me, life would drag on as ever, with me locked into drifting from flat to flat and working in dead-end jobs, only escaping for a few hours through casual drug use. Eleanor did her best to pick me up and got me a job where she was working as a receptionist. It made a change from packing up French fries and I thought that perhaps things might look up if I could find my own place.

I had my deposit for a flat in Scunthorpe when Mum asked to have lunch with me. It was something we'd do from time to time under Dad's careful monitoring – checking when she'd be back and often ringing me to make sure she was there. I didn't mind taking the time out to see her; I wasn't doing as well as I could emotionally and being around her and talking about nothing in particular was its own sort of comfort. She'd ask how I was and I'd say 'fine' then we'd just plough on with the usual chit-chat. So it came as a real surprise to me when she joined me for my lunch break and said, 'Natalia, you have to help me get away from Dad. I need to get out – I can't take any more.'

At first, I didn't say anything. I was confused as she'd always turned down pleas from me and Daiana about leaving. What had happened? The crazy thing was, I didn't ask. I had been let down so many times by my hopes that she would leave that my first thought was that she'd back down again.

So I simply said, 'You need to think about where you'd go.' I thought that by hitting her with the reality of the fact that she had nowhere this might somehow break the spell.

'Fine,' she said. 'It will have to be somewhere not too far away from an ice-rink, for Daniel.'

She and Daiana were taking Daniel's skating seriously and I realised that Elva was trying to make sure that even if her own life was going to be turned upside down, she would do all she could to protect her youngest son.

It was clear to me that she hadn't spoken to Dad. I left to return to work and wondered if this time she was serious and that she was finally ready to take charge of her life. Within a few days, she called me to come to Cleethorpes with her. It was just supposed to be a day out but, in fact, she was house-hunting. It seemed unbelievable to me, but I went with her and we had a lovely day. We looked through the local paper, at jobs and flats to rent, and her spirits were high. In her mind at least, her plans were coming together.

We saw an advert for flats in a new development, Victoria Mills. The mill was a vast old red-brick industrial building that overlooked Alexandra Dock. It was impressive; a landmark for miles around, and the flats inside were well laid out and ready to move into. Mum fell in love with it there and then. She viewed a small two-bedroom apartment for rent, perfect for her and Daniel. And she then talked excitedly about the possibility that I could move into the same building. By now, I'd gone from being sceptical about

Mum's ability to ever break away to being quietly hopeful that it really would happen. The more I watched her face light up as she talked through her plans, the more certain I grew that this time she would leave. And why not? It could be a fresh start for all of us.

Mum told Daiana, and she and her husband said they would help out by hiring a van once a date was set. Throughout this, we all understood that there was no way that Dad could be told. I lived in fear that Daniel might let it slip or that Bruno would suspect something and begin wearing Elva down. At the back of my mind I felt that if he did guess something was afoot, he'd go crazy. He'd stop Mum working for sure, believing that it was the people she was mixing with that was the problem, not the years of coercion and abuse from him. As Mum worked to arrange the move, getting Daniel a place at a new school, signing the lease and so on, I would call home in the morning and ask that she came to lunch or shopping with me. That was the best way to keep Dad from suspecting anything. The moving-out day was planned for 26 April 1997. It was like a military operation, but we all pulled together, knowing that only by leaving Dad entirely, would Mum have any chance of getting on with her life. I lay in bed and thought about it. She was only 47 and faced another lifetime of being demoralised by Dad, who would never change in his need to dominate her. I think she thought about the prospect of old age with him with genuine fear; it was now or never.

Daniel wasn't told that although he would have to go to a new school, his skating would go on as normal. The sad thing was that even though he was a young child, in his eyes, he could look at you with a terrible maturity – he'd seen so much. He was afraid of Dad and despised him, so he was happy to leave too. I felt some guilt over Daniel's loss of innocence. Although I hadn't told him about the rape, I had confided in him too much over the years and treated him as a confidant, and I'm not sure that I should have. Often I felt that he was all I had in the world but it can't have been healthy for him. I had made him promises too, a thousand times, telling him that I would buy stuff I knew I couldn't afford or that I would take him away – I just wanted to see his face light up with the idea that things could be different. I never faced the reality of what it meant to let him down time and time again.

I remember the time he caught me smoking in the garden after my return from the hostel. He snuck up on me and asked, 'What's that?'

'Just a cigarette,' I said.

'Let me try it,' said Daniel. 'If you don't, I'll tell Mum and Dad.'

So I ended up watching my 9-year-old brother, putting a cigarette to his lips. I should have refused, but I honestly didn't have the strength. Away from Dad, I hoped that Daniel would have a second chance at childhood too. Mum was moving out on a Saturday. Dad had a shift at work from 2pm to 10pm and so she knew what her window was. How she carried on that morning with Dad, making sure that everything seemed normal, I can't imagine. Once he had left for work, she hurriedly packed and took the basics of what she and Daniel would need while we waited for her.

It was less than a 30-mile journey to the new flat, but somehow it felt so much more. My heart was in my mouth the whole day, fearing that Dad had only been pretending to be in the dark and that he'd storm in at any moment.

But he knew nothing. We set off by teatime and I can only imagine his face when he came home to an empty house. He would have shouted out for Mum and when no reply came, he would have grown angry that she hadn't replied. He must have felt rage when he realised that his wife and son had disappeared, leaving only a note saying not to try and find them. There was no way that he was going to let them just walk out of his life but that first wave of powerlessness would have been new to him, a realisation of everything he'd ever feared, and he would have reacted in only one way: rage.

Over in Cleethorpes, the scene could not have been more of a contrast. Mum was elated, nervous, but joyful that it had all gone so well. They couldn't move in until the Monday so we found a B&B for them. Daniel was pretty relaxed about the whole upheaval. I remember him asking for some toy or other, but Mum said he couldn't have it as she had to be careful about money. I barked at him, saying that he should not be so selfish, and poor Daniel just piped down.

I wanted to move into a flat in Victoria Mills too but one was not available for another week or so. When I could move in, I would be sharing the flat with a friend of Daiana's. In the meantime, I set up a campbed next to Mum's. Mum would have to wait for proper beds to be delivered and it was a bit like a camping holiday. As she slept one night, I remember watching her and from nowhere the thought came to me, 'This is what Mum would look like if she was dead.' It was the oddest thing. I don't know why it came to me and it took a while before I could shake it off. Perhaps it was just the stress of the move leaving me. I had imagined the worst and now Mum would have a chance to live again.

Dad called Daiana several times but she said she had no idea where Mum was. He went to Daniel's school and to the ice-rink that Daniel went to, but Mum had made the switch and so he was clueless as to where to turn next. He finally reached me and I agreed to go and see him. As I walked into the old house, it was something of a shock. Dad was in the front room crying, something I'd never witnessed before.

He said between sobs, 'Natalia, I just want to speak to your mother. I love her, I want her to come home.'

'Bad luck,' I said. 'I have no sympathy for you. You deserve it.'

'Please, Natalia,' he went on, 'I just want to talk to her.'

'Well, I don't know where she is,' I said calmly, despite Dad pulling me towards him, as if I was going to sit on his knee like a little girl.

'Try Hull, she might be there,' I said flippantly. I felt nothing for him; he'd brought all this on himself. I walked away and didn't look back.

My one fear was that he could turn up and make a scene but in truth, Mum's optimism made it hard for me to worry for too long. She just bloomed. It was as if a burden that had hung around her neck for so many years had been lifted. I always thought she would be happier away from Dad but I had no idea just how much she would change.

It was as if she was finally taking a breath and it altered the way she looked almost instantly. Her weight started to drop off, her eyes shone and she smiled more than I'd ever known. Simple tasks that used to be a chore were suddenly a whole new way to have fun, like food shopping. Years before, I might have been reluctantly dragged around a supermarket, half-sulking, but now it was different. We'd plan a meal and spend most of the time talking, laughing and sharing our thoughts.

Part of me was shocked, but I don't think Mum realised. It was as if I had never truly known her. The woman who'd raised me had been masked by depression and now her real self emerged. She would say and do things that I would never have believed. I can remember being out with her and a good-looking guy walked past us. He was in great shape but I think my jaw hit the floor when I heard Mum say, 'Wow, he's someone you wouldn't mind getting your hands on!' She burst out laughing, in part because of my expression – I was shocked – and partly because she enjoyed saying something outrageous.

She laughed easily and relished every hour we spent together. I felt I was finally getting to know my mother. She'd make me laugh. I remember window shopping with her and she asked, 'Natalia, have you got any cigarettes?'

'No,' I said, knowing how much she disapproved of smoking.

'Oh, go on, just light one up for me,' she said, 'I want to try one.'

I got one out and lit it up, handing it to Mum, stunned at what she'd asked for.

'No, it's for you, silly,' Mum said, 'I can tell you're dying for a fag. Just don't smoke in the flat, that's all.'

There was my Mum, abused all those years but in front of me now, a happy and a complete person, and teasing her daughter because she knew her better than she knew herself.

I was honest with her. I'd pour my heart out about stupid men I'd been seeing and random stuff that bothered me. I could tell her about anything about the disastrous relationships I was trying to get out of and she'd listen to me and make me feel that everything would be OK. She was so patient; she never condemned me and did her best to advise me, but in the back of my mind, I did wonder what use it was as I thought she'd led such a sheltered life, only knowing Dad. It was Mum who said that I was a born fighter, that I had a heart of gold but that I felt alone and so that made me fight all the more, even at the risk of losing people who loved me like David. She also warned me that I was a girl who had to learn the hard way. She often said, 'If you tell Natalia that fire will burn her, she won't listen. She'll put her hand in the flames and watch herself burn. She has to find out for herself.'

I could be fierce but I was also brittle, masking a lot of the hurt I felt. Once, emotionally raw, I asked her why she let Dad hit me. She said, 'Natalia, what could I do?' And she'd look so dejected again, just as she had at home, and I'd feel terrible. She thought that if she had intervened, everything would have been worse. To cross Dad was insane, only driving his anger up a notch higher. She had waited for his rage to blow over, believing that was the way to limit the damage. But it wasn't my way, and Mum knew it. In that way, I thought, we would always be different; I was probably always a worry to her, but I did not know that when she looked at me, she saw more than an angry young woman: she saw herself.

At that point, what concerned Mum was re-building her relationship with her children and finding a job. She had been for a job interview to work at the local job centre. She was encouraging me to go for a position there too and the idea of working alongside her sounded fun – I thought we'd have a ball. Although she was nervous about the interview, I saw her dressed in a suit and she looked fantastic. I wished her luck, and said that I was sure she'd do well and sure enough she did. She was thrilled when she was through to the next round and when she learned that I had managed to get an interview for another job there, she just glowed. Beyond work, the other things she wanted were for Daniel to keep skating and for Daiana, Emmanuele and me to be part of her new life. But there was always a shadow: she knew Dad was waiting. Waiting for his chance to find her.

Daiana was their go-between; she was very protective of Mum and wanted to keep them apart. I wanted nothing to do with him, even his name would cause me to flare up. Why would Mum bother? If he was upset, good, serves him right for all the years he made us suffer. But she was calm and tried to make me understand that even if she was no longer able to survive being married to him, that didn't mean he wasn't our father and that he still had the right to see Daniel. Daiana had given Mum her mobile phone and it was on that number that he reached her – I think it was just a lucky guess on his part. He was tearful and sorry, rather than furious. That made sense – if he'd kicked off with fire and brimstone, Mum would have found it easier to put down the phone. Instead, he pleaded with her. Mum tried to be mature and clear in her dealings with him and she asked him to accept that their marriage was over. She said she would not prevent him seeing Daniel, but as for the rest of us, we were old enough to make our own decisions.

She was making decisions for herself too. Once she left Dad, she never visited the Jehovah's church again. She asked Daniel if he wanted to go but he said no, and that was that. I don't think her decision to leave was because she no longer had faith – I think she believed in God but the church she was pushed into was Bruno's decision. He'd made her convert to Catholicism, and then become a Jehovah's Witness. Neither bore much resemblance to the quiet and reflective faith Elva had; it was her own spiritual journey. I saw other changes in her – for example, in her attitude towards my flatmate. He was gay and previously Mum would have been very subdued, knowing how violently her church and Bruno disapproved of homosexuality. Now, she was judging my flatmate on his own merits – who he shared a bed with, she felt, wasn't her concern. He would never have known that she'd lived around homophobia all her life.

Dad called her to say that there was mail for her to pick up, and wouldn't it be nice for Daniel if he could see his old friends. Daniel had missed them; he'd been used to running out of the back of the house and playing safely with the same group of boys he had known since he was tiny. Mum thought about it and agreed to call by with him. She didn't want any more acrimony. She'd spent a lifetime coping with Dad's bitter attempts to control her and she didn't want to be responsible for turning their split into a new battlefield. She wanted Daniel to be happy and not feel as if his father was the enemy. Her one stumbling block was me. It was a Friday night and I was getting ready for a night out. I picked out what I was going to wear and let Mum in for a chat while I got ready. I ran a bath and Mum sat down and told them about her decision to visit Dad, with Daniel, the next day. After putting aside my objections and her own fears that Dad would harm her, she promised to take me with her.

I went out and partied. I partied so hard that even though I made it through the front door, I had to crash on the sofa for a while. Somehow I got into bed but when I woke up a few hours later, I was still exhausted. I climbed back onto the sofa and was soon sound asleep. I slept so heavily that I had no idea that Mum had come down from her flat with Daniel and had seen me through the window. I didn't hear Mum tell him that she'd prefer to leave me so that I could sleep on. I didn't hear her, didn't sense that she was there, that she needed me. If I'd woken up, if I'd been in my bedroom instead of the front room, would that have made any difference? Would she have knocked and taken me with her? As it was, she didn't knock and I would never see my sweet and caring mother alive again.

CHAPTER SEVEN

THE LAST DAY

My flatmate went pale. 'Natalia, it's the police. Oh my God!' Both of us were dope smokers and although we didn't have much dope in the flat, the sight of the police at the intercom, asking for me, was enough to make us both panic.

I told my flatmate that I'd get the stash and run up to Mum's flat until they had gone. For half an hour, I waited at Mum's, realising now that she had left without me, and made some calls. I called her on her mobile but there was no answer. I tried the house, but no one would pick up; I called my grandmother with no luck and then my sister. I couldn't get anyone to pick up. I called Daiana at work and they told me that she had had to leave suddenly. It was then that a new fear washed over me. I thought about Mum and what she'd said: 'Natalia, I think if your father sees me again, he will kill me.' My mind started racing. He'd done it. He'd killed her. He doesn't have a gun, so what would he do? He's stabbed her.

I ran back to my flat and there was a piece of paper with a telephone number on it, for the police station.

'It's not the pot, is it?' I asked my flatmate.

'I don't know. All they asked for was you and said that they needed to talk to you about your mum,' he said. 'Do you think she's been in an accident?'

'No,' was my reply, and I was surprised how calm I sounded. 'I'm going to call them now.' I rang and all the desk sergeant would tell me was that two police officers were on their way.

It was probably only 15 minutes but in that time, I felt my life slow down and shudder to a halt. I could hardly breathe and I lay between two worlds: I knew and yet I did not know. My flatmate offered me a cup of coffee but I couldn't reply. Eventually, the intercom buzzed and I heard footsteps approach the door. I opened it to see a male and a female officer, both in uniform. They looked grave and held their helmets in their hands. I don't think I have ever studied a face so intently as that policeman's and yet if you asked me to remember anything about him now, I couldn't. He was asking me my name, for proof of my identity; for my home address and the names of my mother and father.

I gave all the information mechanically and then said simply: 'He's killed her hasn't he? He's stabbed her to death.' It was a statement, not a question, but I wanted at that moment for the police officers to step forward and tell me no, I was wrong and not to worry. I desperately wanted to get to Mum, to make sure she was OK. I needed to see Daniel – he mustn't know; I wanted Daiana, I wanted her to tell me what was happening and why and how it would stop. All they did was quickly look at each other and the male officer said: 'Natalia, I'm very sorry, your mother is dead.'

I felt nausea and cold fear; a collision of emotions and questions. I was a scared little girl again. I wanted Mum to walk through the door and say that she was fine and to tell me that I was just being silly. But in the back of my mind, a cold voice said, 'Come on, Natalia, you know what he's done. It's over.' I became hysterical. Why wouldn't the police help me? Through my tears and anguish they were talking about making a statement. They weren't going to take me to my family, they said they wouldn't until I spoke to them and gave them my statement. How could they be so cruel? I couldn't understand what they were saying or what they wanted from me but I understood clearly that all my tears and pleas were getting me nowhere. They'd get what they wanted. I had to be a good girl. I'd learned the hard way that my protests couldn't help me.

They took me to a police station in Grimsby and into an interview room, where a tape recorder was switched on and I was questioned. 'Tell us about your dad, did he and your mum argue at all?' It was like a flood: I had been drowning in all I felt and now it spewed forth. I called him jealous and possessive, a bully and a man who would do anything to control his wife and children. I told them how he had stopped her having friends, how he'd kept her from working or had stalked her and made her life a misery when she had; how he thought all wives should obey their husbands or face punishment. How could he have done it? All she had ever done was look after him and us; she was so kind and deserved a life without him and now he had made orphans of us all. By killing her, he was dead to me too. He was evil. And on and on I railed, not realising that much of what I said would be brought up in court; and used against my dad.

I was frantic and needed to see my brother and sister. I announced I was leaving and that I'd hitchhike to Scunthorpe if I had to. But I was stopped and told that a car would take me to the station in Scunthorpe where my family was waiting. Dad included. I hadn't thought about him; all I wanted was to see Daniel. He was the first to run up to me at the station, saying, 'Natalia, I've been in a real police car with a siren and everything!'

I looked up at the WPC who was with him and whispered, 'Does he know?'

'Yes,' she said simply, and looked at us both with pity.

'And then I was allowed to sit and turn things on and off and press buttons,' Daniel carried on, and he was still talking as we walked in to see Daiana and Emmanuele.

Everyone looked in shock and no one knew what to say. There had been tears but I don't think the reality of what had happened had sunk in with any of us, and in part, no one wanted to become hysterical in front of Daniel. He was 9 years old and in one afternoon he had lost both parents. Daiana had borne the brunt of events as they unfolded. She had been the one to get Dad's phone call demanding that she come and take care of my brothers; she had been the one to talk to Daniel and she was one who was asked to identify Mum's body.

As the eldest, she was expected to deal with the family and Dad's brutality as she always had. My heart should have gone out to her but I was numb with shock and couldn't begin to focus on how to help her. She must have realised that Emmanuele, who'd been living with Dad and seemed more bewildered than ever, had nowhere to go. Neither did Daniel.

Emmanule asked, 'Where will we go now?'

'You'll both come home with me,' Daiana said steadily.

I realised that she had little enough room to house me as well but part of me silently cried, 'Why haven't you asked me?' Of course, in practical terms, I had the flat to return to, but at that moment I had never felt so alone. The crisis would not pull the Aggiano children together; it was the start of events that would rip us apart.

A police sergeant came in and I asked him, 'Where's Dad?'

'He's being interviewed,' he replied.

'And when can I see him?' I asked.

'You won't see him,' he said, and his whole manner was pretty abrupt. But it was nothing compared to the look on my sister's face.

'Well, I want to see him,' I said, coldly. 'I want to talk to him.'

'Well, you can't,' the sergeant said, his annoyance evident.

At this point I lost it. I started yelling that they had no right to stop me talking to my father. In my mind, I wanted to see him and ask him what had happened. Maybe it had been an accident; after all, he did love Mum and even though I had hated my dad for longer than I could remember, I still could not believe that he could look into my mum's eyes and decide to murder her. Perhaps the whole thing had been a mistake, perhaps she'd had an accident cooking for him... I know how irrational that sounds now. I had believed that my dad was capable of murder, and now I didn't. My mind couldn't hold together all I was being told and the possibility that Mum wouldn't be coming home with me that night. If she had cut herself with a knife when cooking, perhaps she would be OK after all and then all of this would go away.

But the sergeant angrily insisted that I couldn't talk to Dad and this pushed every instinct I had, the instincts that kept me alive all those years, battling Dad's brutality and forcing me to carry on with my life even after being attacked. That sergeant should not have said 'no'. If he had calmly told me, maybe later, or tomorrow and I'll be there to help you, who knows how my life would have turned out? I honestly believe that if he hadn't made me fight to see Dad that night, I would not have seen him at all and my life would have taken a very different turn.

Daiana was horrified. She could not understand why I would want any contact with the man who had tried to destroy our lives and had succeeded in destroying our mother's. He was a monster in her eyes. But another police officer, PC Broughton, interrupted the argument and said, 'Look, here's a piece of paper, write him a note and I'll make sure he gets it once the interview has concluded, and then you can come and see him tomorrow.' I thanked him; he seemed the only one in uniform able to understand part of what we were going through. He handed me a piece of paper and a pen. What could I write? What could I possibly write? Everyone was staring at me as I sat down. This is what I wrote:

Dad, I want to see you but they have said that I can't. I know
what you have done but it doesn't matter. I love you. Please
say that you will see me – your daughter.

To read it, it sounds callous to say 'it doesn't matter'. But as
I wrote, I knew that I had to get to see him so that I could
learn the truth. If I had been angry, if I condemned him, he
might have refused and I would be left without answers. I
knew I had little time to write and those were the words
that came.

Daiana was getting everyone ready to leave the station. I
said that I wanted to go and see Helen, to tell her. As I
walked out, I realised that one of our old neighbours, Paula,
was a friend of Mum's and she too should be told what was
happening. She lived opposite the house and can't have
failed to notice that something was wrong. I walked down
the street where I had grown up and stared in disbelief at the
police cordon and officers standing in front of our house. I
knocked on Paula's door. She was in tears and told me that
she had seen the ambulance remove Mum's body. She told
me that I would always be welcome at her home and to
please, keep in touch and let her know if there was anything
she could do. She asked if I wanted to stay there but I said
no. I couldn't imagine sitting in a house across the road from
Mum's house, so I thanked her and walked on to Helen's.

Just walking was proving hard. How was it that
everything could have changed and yet there was no sign,
as I headed to Helen's, that anything had at all? People were
watching television, walking dogs and going into their
houses with shopping bags. Why were they doing that?

How *could* they? Perhaps they hadn't realised what a terrible thing had happened because if they had, they wouldn't just stand and chat. Yet part of me knew that this was exactly how it was going to be. It was just a headline, something that gave the neighbourhood a real shock but something that would not interrupt the day-to-day for too long. It's other people's misfortune you think, and turn to the next thing. I wanted to scream. I sensed that if I stopped walking, I would collapse. But I kept on walking, on autopilot, placing one foot in front of the other, with no idea how to contain all I felt.

Helen did all she could. She wanted me to stay but I asked if she would take me back to the flat. One or two others came, too. I don't really remember who, and my flatmate was there. I could barely speak. Only a week or so earlier, Mum had given me a candle. I've always loved candles and the one she gave me was beautiful. Too beautiful to burn, I'd told her – I'd keep it forever instead. Now I sat, and lit the candle, and watched the small, flickering flame. My friends tried to talk to me but I wouldn't look away from the candle. I can remember someone saying, 'Seriously, I think she's losing it.' I couldn't respond.

My mum had been the one loving parent in my life and she had been snatched away. Being with her over the last few weeks had been an inspiration. My beautiful fragile Mum, who had only ever tried her best to love those around her – even me, who stole from her, lied to her and called her a failure. She had loved me and, yes, I was losing it: I had lost everything.

I don't remember going to bed. I do recall waking, and that split second before I remembered everything. It was true. I felt a roar of pain and I lay there willing my own life away. I could not get through this day. As if my mind was testing me, a thought came: But you said you'd see Dad. Dad. My father, the killer. Would I go? I stood in the shower and tried to unscramble what had happened at the station and what I had said. I realised I did want to see him. I needed to look him in the eye, to make him face me and see if he could stand the shame; to see if he could live with himself once he'd seen his daughter before him. He'd always said he loved Mum, always said he loved his children, so how could he destroy us all and sit there imagining he could carry on? He had not just taken Mum's life, he had taken the knife to us all. Let him deal with that.

I arrived at the station at around 11am and was surprised to see Emmanuele waiting there too. He hardly acknowledged me. I could see that he was not coping and his grief seemed to add to his confusion. He didn't want to talk. I told the desk sergeant why we were there and was told to wait. I was also told that Dad had been charged with murder and that he would be held at the station until Monday, when he'd be taken to Lincoln prison. He'd have to go to a magistrates' court first and the prison would be where he would be held on remand until he would stand trial. Words like 'murder', 'remand' and 'trial' were so familiar from reading newspapers and watching TV, but I still could not believe this was happening to us, our family. It didn't comfort me, the idea that the judicial wheels were turning; it only added to my sense of hopelessness. As for the police, they were going through the motions – the procedure necessary to clear up a crime and restore order. There would be no restoration for us: we had been torn apart, our hearts and our hope destroyed; we were motherless and fatherless. And the police, courts and lawyers seemed to be ticking boxes, working through a process that was far, far removed from what we felt and knew.

And so I sat in silence. What was I doing there? How could I face him? All the resolve and anger I felt earlier that morning was now wrecked by confusion. I was a little girl again and I began to tremble. Perhaps if I saw him, I would break the spell and the bad things would no longer be true. I was staring at the ground when an officer came and told me it was time to see Dad. I felt sick with nerves as we were walked to the holding area. I was told that I would be able to see and hear Dad, but not touch him as he would be behind a Perspex window. Much of what I was being told washed over me and I was only dimly aware of Emmanuele walking along behind me. A door was opened and we were led into a room. I saw Dad and everything I felt was shattered. He was sitting in a white plastic suit, and he was crying. He looked so small and pathetic. I could hardly believe that this was the man who had dominated my life, who had haunted me and my attempts to be free of him.

But before I could think what to say, Emmanule erupted into anger and started to furiously smash the Perspex and scream abuse. He was in a rage the like of which I'd never seen. I had been used to him lashing out when I was a kid but that was at me, never at Dad, and this was very different. He was overcome by the horror of what had happened and could not cope any more. I felt sure he would smash through the glass. I could not believe that it would hold up to his kicks and punches. I screamed for the police to come back. Dad was crying and saying, 'I'm sorry, I'm so sorry,' over and over again. Two officers rushed in and I said, 'Please take him away. I have to speak to my father, please stop him.' They hauled Emmanuele out of the room, still kicking and howling.

The silence that followed was like a blow. Dad was still sobbing and I was left standing, unable to think of what to say. I knew I had to take control, so I sat down. Dad could not look at me.

'Dad, you have to tell me what happened,' I said. 'You have to tell me the truth, because if you lie to me, I swear to God you will never see me again as long as you live. I don't care how painful the truth is. If it is the truth I will find a way to cope with it, but if you lie, we are finished. Do you understand me?'

He looked up and was silent but then he said, 'I promise you, Natalia.'

He had made me a promise before: he'd promised never to hit me if I came home from the hostel and he had stuck to his word. I knew that he would keep his word this time, too. What I didn't know, was where the hunt for the truth would lead me. If I had known, would I still have demanded it? For it left me with the burden of unfinished horror.

CHAPTER EIGHT

A LIFE WITH GRIEF

Dad told me about the note a police officer gave him: he was sure it was from Daiana. He said he could not believe his eyes when he saw it was me who had walked in: the bad daughter, the daughter who hated him, the daughter that wished him dead.

I listened with my hands folded in front of me. I wasn't there to hear about his surprise.

'Tell me what happened,' I said bluntly.

'I'm sorry, so very sorry…' he'd begun to cry again.

'You've said that,' I cut in. 'Tell me what happened. I want to know why.'

'You have to understand,' he said, looking directly into my eyes, 'I had to do it, Natalia. God told me that I had to. I had to kill your mother's body to save her soul.'

I stated at him, unblinking. I had heard Dad's religious

ramblings for years but I could not believe that he felt this was at all plausible.

'Dad,' I said, 'I can't believe you. You thought it was for you to decide. It was you who picked up the knife.'

His stare was as steady as my own. 'Natalia, your mother took her wedding vows. To sin this way meant that she would be cast into hell. I love your mother; she is the only woman I have ever loved. I had to save her, I did not want her to suffer.'

I was incredulous. 'What do you mean, suffer? You stabbed her!'

'I freed her,' he said, calmly. 'Jesus came to me and presented me with three options. He said that either Mum must come home and repent. Or if I let her stay away, then I would be to blame for letting her spirit be sent to purgatory, or I could take her life and save her spirit. I told her, "This is your final warning," but she said she would not come home. I told her that the hedge of protection had been taken away from her and she was vulnerable to the Devil. I told her that God would curse her and the children. I had to save her.

'I will be with her again. I am not going to eat now, Natalia, you should know that. I am going to starve myself. It is the most painful way that you can die and it is what I want to do.'

'I think that's probably for the best,' I said, starkly. And I meant it. Why should he live? He had taken away Mum and tried to justify it through some twisted belief in his God. Let him go. He told me again how sorry he was for how his children had been left and he talked about how much he loved Mum.

I couldn't listen to any more and so I got up. 'Please Natalia, will you visit me again?'

It was part of the bargain I had made. 'Yes,' I said, and left.

Outside, my head was spinning and I felt nauseous again. I hadn't eaten, but I didn't want to. I just wanted to walk and try and get on top of every emotion and thought that smashed through me. I was crying but the tears gave me no release: I wanted to see my mum.

My plan was to get back to Mum's flat. I needed to be with her. Once there, I could hardly bear to see her few possessions, waiting for their owner, impassive. I picked up one of her dolls: she had a collection of porcelain dolls and I knew which one was her favourite. I held it and the tears came again. I don't know how long I sat there. Time is fractured by grief. Sometimes you do not believe you will get through the next minute, just moving through time seems impossible. Then you will be told that it is late and that you haven't eaten, but all sense of rhythm to the day and night has been lost. You move through it without understanding.

I took the doll and put it in Mum's window – I don't know why, even to this day. I also wrote Mum a poem and put it with the doll with some flowers. What I wrote could never chart all I felt but it was the start of realising all I had lost. I wrote:

Somebody listened, somebody knows, about
  All the highs and all my lows,
  When someone listens, it's easy to see.
  It's alright to be just me.

That mask of mine is now removed
The wounds I have now feel soothed
She makes me feel like I will win
My past life had been no sin
I feel the fighter inside me now
The winner inside me will take her bow
Somebody listened, somebody heard,
That's all I wanted, was to be heard.
And my dearest mother did.

I love you. Please watch over me.
Natalia xxxx

Mum had done so much for me, and even more so in the last few weeks of her life. She had made me believe that I could be OK again and now I needed to see her, to thank her and be with her. Her body was kept at the hospital morgue. Daiana had been there to identify her. I wanted to sit with her now that all the doctors, police and mortuary staff had finished cataloguing what they had found – she would need someone there. I called the police station and asked their advice. I was happy to hear that it was PC Broughton, our family liaison officer, who would pick me up and take me to Daiana's house. I wanted to see the family, particularly Daniel, and tell them that I was visiting Mum. When we got there, Emmanuele opened the door; Daiana was out, starting to make the funeral arrangements. Emmanuele didn't speak; he disappeared and left me with Daniel and PC Broughton. Daniel wanted to know where I was going, but I hesitated. He asked again and so I told him.

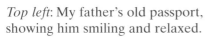

Top left: My father's old passport, showing him smiling and relaxed.

Top right: My school photo, aged 7, taken when violence at home was already a feature of my life.

Above: My parents at a wedding reception. When they first met, Mum was a gregarious and attractive young woman. As the years went by, depression overcame her, and it was only once she left Dad that her spark returned.

Bottom right: Elva and Bruno standing in the garden of our family house.

Top left: On my roller skates near the family home in Scunthorpe. Despite my father's awful behaviour, there were occasional snatches of happiness.

Top right: With Daniel as a toddler. Mum took the picture, but in a few years, she would be taken from us.

Bottom left: My grandmother with Daniel.

Bottom right: Daniel and I have been through so much together, and I am so proud of him.

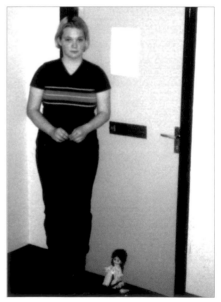

Top: The afternoon the Aggiano house was turned into a crime scene.

Bottom left: Police were stationed in the back garden while evidence was gathered. The room in which Mum died is directly behind the officer.

Bottom right: Standing outside Mum's flat a short while after her death when I felt the force of her presence bidding me goodbye.

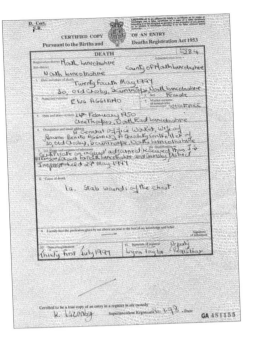

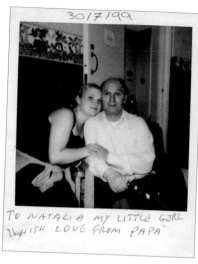

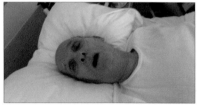

Top left: My mother's death certificate, showing the cause of death as stab wounds to the heart.

Top right: A Polaroid taken of Dad and me on a visit I paid him when he was in Rampton Secure Hospital. You can see his message to his 'little girl' at the bottom.

Bottom left: A shot of me and Bruno once his chemotherapy was over.

Bottom right: Is this what a killer looks like? Dad's illness shattered everything. He was my last link to Mum and the thought of losing that terrified me.

'I'll come too,' he said.

I looked at the officer and said, 'I don't think you are allowed to come Daniel, sorry.'

'There's no reason why he can't,' PC Broughton said. 'Children are allowed.'

I looked at Daniel, who was staring at me intently.

'Please, Natalia,' he said, 'I want to come.'

I agreed. I didn't feel I had the right to deny him his chance to say goodbye to his mum, and so we set off together.

The staff at the hospital were kind. They were used to dealing with the bereaved but I could see a certain curiosity in people's eyes. Mum's body being removed from the house had been on the news and in the local newspaper. Daniel and I were the children of a murderer and people, no matter how kind their intentions, couldn't help but stare.

I had seen the news footage of our house, of the police and ambulance crew but still it did not seem real. In fact, watching it had made it seem all the more unreal. But this was different. We were led down a corridor and a flight of stairs to a room set at the side of the morgue where we would see Mum's lifeless body. A door opened onto a small room which held Mum's temporary coffin. She was covered up with a sheet from her neck down; all we could see were her hands and face. It was so odd to see Mum without her glasses – she always wore her glasses. I put my hand out to stroke her cheek and then froze. It was then that it hit me: This wasn't Mum – Elva's skin always blazed warm, even on the coldest of days, I could hug her and feel the heat pour out from her skin. Now her face was cold to the touch. It was wrong, something was wrong. This wasn't Mum, and she wasn't going to wake up.

I sat down with Daniel and was alone with my thoughts. It was hard to feel anything coherent. I looked at Mum's face. It looked nothing at all like the face I had studied only two weeks ago as she slept. It wasn't an expression I had ever seen on her face before. I had grown up accustomed to seeing Mum look anxious or sad, but now she seemed angry; she looked as if she wanted to say something. Daniel stepped over to the side of Mum's coffin and stared at her intently. He seemed puzzled more than anything and then he reached his hands out to Mum's face. I stood next to him and was shocked to see that he was trying to open her eyes.

'Daniel, what are you doing?' I burst out.

'I want to see Mum's eyes,' he said. 'I just want to see Mum with her eyes open.'

He was calm, but growing confused. Clearly he thought that if he helped her open her eyes, then she would sit back up, alive once more. How do you explain death to a 9-year-old, to a boy who was inseparable from his mother? I held his hands and said quietly, 'You can't do that, Daniel.' He stood for a little while and I could barely look at him. His face was one of anguish and confusion: Mum loved him, so why wouldn't she wake up?

More in an effort to try and make things as bearable as possible for Daniel, and at a loss for what else to do, I began to talk. I tried to tell Mum what was happening to us all, that Daniel was OK, and that Daiana was doing her best to look after us all. What I wanted to say was that I could not do this without her, but I couldn't with my baby brother there.

I talked and talked, not really sure of all I was saying but somehow, finding it the best place to be. Mum had listened to me over the years, usually with a look of worry as her daughter seemed so angry with her lot, but over the last few weeks, we had found each other again. I'd found the real Mum and she'd helped me start to be the real Natalia. I liked her so much. Now he'd taken her from us forever. This was the hardest thing of all. I would never get to know the woman who was my real mum now. She had only just begun to live and like a vengeful God, he had destroyed her.

I didn't want to break down in front of Daniel. Mum's words came back to me: 'Natalia, I love your dad. I am not *in* love with him but I love him for who he is, not what he does. Just like you, you are my daughter and you have done wrong in your life but I love you for *you*, not what you do.'

Could she still have felt that way when he bore down on her, thrusting the kitchen knife into her time and time again? No. And I could not feel love for him now. No love is great enough to overcome such horror. Where was her loving God then? Murdered by my dad and his Old Testament wrath. This was nothing to do with God: it was nonsense. What had driven him was fear. Here was an old man, terrified to be left without his wife, a wife who was clearly thriving once she was out of harm's way. I was glad Dad had decided to starve himself to death but if there was any justice, I hoped they would not be reconciled in any afterlife.

It was time to leave. I was afraid of all I was feeling and I wanted to get Daniel back to the house. When we got there, Daiana was waiting and she was furious. She could not believe that I had been stupid and insensitive enough to take Daniel. She was terrified that he would go into shock now that he had seen Mum. I tried to explain what the police officer had said but she didn't want to hear it. I was worn out and could hardly cope with another row. I said that it was a good thing to do, to see her. Daiana exploded. 'How *can* it be good? I *had* to see her — her hair was still wet, she had been sliced open and pulled apart in there. You have no idea, *no idea*, Natalia!'

I was confused at first. It took me a moment to realise she wasn't talking about the house and Dad, but the doctors at the morgue, and surely she would not have seen Mum's lacerated body? But grief was overwhelming her and she was right — she alone had to say yes, that's my mother as she lay on a mortuary slab. The full effect of all she had seen and was being charged with coping with was too much. She was housing her brothers, informing family and friends as well as making funeral arrangements. Her marriage was under serious strain and all she needed was me, her wayward sister, to do something she would not have dreamt of and this was the trigger point for her to detonate.

But the biggest rift of all was my decision to go back and see Bruno again. Daiana could not believe that I would, and in doing so, offer comfort to him. I didn't see it as comfort. Perhaps I was naïve but I had offered little other than harsh questioning and the promise that I would only come back if he told me the truth. At this point, I honestly believed my dad would not live beyond a month as his resolve to die seemed absolute. So I was left with an even greater rift with my sister than ever before. Carrying that as well as all that had happened was too much. I left Daiana's house.

It is hard to focus on the events of those days immediately after Mum's death. I can remember that Dad was moved to Lincoln prison, I think after the weekend, and was to appear in the magistrates court that Tuesday, to have the charges against him read out. This was part of court procedure but he was brought back again on the Friday to be told that he would be held on remand, back at Lincoln, until the date for his trial was set. It was then that Dad's solicitor told the court that Bruno was on a hunger strike. This set the press into a frenzy again and they tracked me down at Victoria Mills, looking for a quote. I told them that I didn't think he'd last another week. I didn't want to see him in court but I had promised to visit him in prison. I had written him a letter and all my rage for what he had done spilled into it. I told him that I hated him. He was soon moved to the hospital wing and was refusing food.

Behind closed doors, I struggled with the fact that I didn't want to see him at court but that I had promised to see him in prison.

A journalist contacted me as it was said that Bruno had been moved to the hospital wing and told that unless he ate, he had only ten days or so to live. I said that I didn't want Dad to be force fed, I thought they should let him go. He knew the enormity of his crime and I thought that he should be left to die. This dragged on until day 15 and I felt the next call would be to say that he was dead.

It was around this time that something happened to me that to this day I cannot explain. I had got back to the flat at Victoria Mills and it was about 6pm. I had not been eating properly but had no interest in cooking. Even though it was early, I was exhausted and crawled into bed. I fell asleep straightaway but I had no idea for how long. I woke up and looked at the clock: it said nine. I'd slept right through. I got up and put the kettle on and sat down on the sofa, next to my cigarettes. I heard the door rattle; it was a very familiar sound as it was a stiff catch that Mum always rattled twice before she managed to open the door. Hearing the rattle, I thought, 'Oh, it's Mum', and said, 'Come in.' It was then that it hit me: It couldn't be Mum. My head swung round to the door in horror.

It didn't open. I stood up. There was something in the room and I was terrified. The room started to spin, but it was not dizziness; it felt as if someone was pulling at my arms and swinging me around. I felt sick with fear and was saying, 'Please stop, *please*, I don't like it.' Then my packet of cigarettes flew off the sofa. I was crying and saying, 'Who is it? Please stop, you are scaring me.' And it stopped. It felt like an energy had drained from the room. I thought, Dad? He must be dead and he's trying to scare me.

I ran out of the flat down to the nearest phone box to call Daiana. I was hysterical and asking if Dad had died. She said no, she was sure he hadn't but that she would check. Luckily for me, my flatmate came walking up the road and he was shocked to see me in such a state. We stayed by the phone and Daiana rang back to say that Dad had not died. Then could it have been Mum? It made no sense and I was badly shaken. My flatmate came back with me. I entered the flat but whatever it was, had gone. I prayed that it would not happen again, and it didn't. But I never felt at peace at Victoria Mills again.

Dad was alive and what was more, the prison called to say that he had accepted a cup of tea. That was extraordinary as he never drank tea, only coffee. But more was to follow: Dad wanted to see us; he'd put in a call to Daiana and me. My sister wouldn't speak to him. The cause of his new interest in life was Mum's funeral arrangements. He'd been told that he would not be allowed to attend. I can barely believe that he thought he would be. But he was slipping further into the delusion that he had 'saved' her. He told me that I had to see him as he had 'something to tell me'. Was it a new confession? Had he been keeping something from me?

The hunger strike was over. He ended it because of his new obsession – Mum's funeral. He was shocked that he would not be allowed to attend. There was no way on earth that we would have allowed it but we were told not to worry as it is prison policy never to allow the accused to attend their alleged victim's funeral. But Dad was determined to send flowers. He called me in to beg me to send flowers to Mum on his behalf. I talked to Daiana, but she refused point blank. Dad was left to plead with me. He was desperate and seemed to think that Elva's peace had something to do with a special message he had to send through his flowers. He asked if I do nothing else for him, to be allowed to send his own bouquet.

I was torn by Dad's pathetic pleading and Daiana's refusal to have any sign of his presence. In my mind, I understood both of them: Daiana was right to despise him, but here was a sick old man, who had destroyed everything he had held dear, clearly mentally unwell. Would his flowers, hidden under my name, *really* matter? But Daiana and I were in no mood for rational discussion and I was to blame as much as her. My insistence on seeing Dad enraged her and now it was my turn to lose my temper. Daiana wanted 'Elva Winfarrah' on the gravestone. I started yelling that there was no way that should happen. To me, she was Elva Aggiano. I did not know her as anything else and we were all Aggianos, like it or not. Daiana wanted to remove all evidence that Bruno had ever existed in Mum's life and this was an obvious step she felt. I was less than reasonable; I screamed at Daiana that I would visit the gravestone every day and write Aggiano on it until she accepted the fact that Mum was not a 'Winfarrah'. 'That's not her,' I wailed.

Ultimately, the compromise was an obvious one. The name that would appear on our mother's gravestone was simply, 'Elva'. But it was a sign of how fragile I was feeling. I was yelling at my sister as if she were Dad, just unable to back down. I felt that so much was now out of my control that Mum's headstone took on great importance. I had lost so much; I could not have Daiana creating a name that meant nothing to me.

We were finding it harder and harder to spend time in each other's company. To Daiana, I could come and go as I pleased while it was she who was left with all the hard detail and decisions. She did not want to be a mother, something she told me a few years ago, and now she found she was mother to a traumatised 9–year–old. Emmanuele had never lived alone and now she had him to cope with, too. The final straw was her younger sister. In her eyes, I was selfish and childish, and had been the source of a lot of antagonism at home, failing to help protect Mum from Dad's rage. And now I was stubbornly keeping in contact with her murderer. It was hardly surprising that she withdrew herself from me emotionally, but I felt more alone than ever and it truly broke my heart.

With Dad out of the hospital wing and back in the regular prison, I had mixed emotions about the fact that he was going to live. It would have been far simpler if he had died; it would have been just in some way and now I worried about the effect his presence would continue to have on us all. I had promised I would visit and of course, I could have refused – after all, what did I owe him? But there was a part of me that hungered for the truth of what happened and wanted to face up to my Dad once and for all. I could understand Daiana when she said, 'He is dead to me. I have no parents.' But I could not fool myself so easily – or at least, doing so did not seem the way I could, or would, cope. I couldn't hide from it. As a child, I couldn't keep my mouth shut when everyone wanted me to; I just couldn't swallow my anger and keep my head down. And it was the same now I could not pretend Dad was dead. While he was still alive, I wanted to deal with how I felt about him head-on and that meant squaring up to him once again.

But my decision to keep contact with him came at a price, and not just at the expense of my relationship with Daiana. I had kept my word and called on my old neighbour, Paula. She opened her door and her face darkened when she saw it was me. She spat at me: 'Your mother would turn in her grave if she knew what you were doing. How *could* you see him?' Her face was contorted with rage and I said nothing. It was such a horrible shock. I turned and walked away, not registering what she was shouting after me.

The horror that people felt by my decision to see Dad was felt elsewhere too. Mum's family was mortified and wouldn't speak to me. Even as I walked down the street, I felt people looking and whispering. It took no time at all for the whole area to know and have an opinion about what I was doing. No one had the guts to ask me outright; I had just become something for people to gossip and shake their heads about. Everyone felt that if their mum had been killed by their dad, they would never even look at him again. But I will tell you honestly, I will never judge anyone's actions if they are dealing with a horrific murder. Because it isn't you and unless it is, your imagination does not even come close to how you would feel. I had lost everything and was trying my best to stay sane and to find a lifeline out of the blackness. And fewer and fewer people were willing to talk to me; some even felt happy to spit at me as I walked by.

I so desperately wanted to talk to Mum. In my head I talked to her a lot and knew that seeing her helped me begin to deal with my grief, even if the relief was temporary. I arranged to see Mum again, as she had now been moved to a Chapel of Rest at the funeral home. It was a better place to be, I thought, as I walked in. Here were people accustomed to grief and to making family feel welcome. I was led to where Mum was but when I walked up to her coffin, I gasped – Mum's face was bruised. I felt a new wave of revulsion: Dad had beaten her. I was shaking but the attendant stepped in saying no, it was part of the process of decay. I was at once relieved, yet horrified. Why not being hit in the face should make me feel better almost makes no sense. But those were days when sense played no part in my existence. I think it was because I understood what it felt like to be punched, but being stabbed was still so far beyond what I could understand that it was unreal. It didn't want her to have been hurt. So silly, of course she had been hurt. I sat and cried.

Decay – that was such a horrid word. She was lying there in front of me; I didn't want her to hear that. Part of me knew Mum wasn't here any more but still I was sure she could hear me. I felt nothing like the sheer force that night in the flat. Mum's spirit wasn't there but still I took comfort from being close to her. I poured out my heart, telling her about Dad and what everyone thought. I asked her to forgive me. I wanted her to let me know if I was doing the right thing. I did not want to add to her hurt. *Was* I doing the right thing? What did she think? I don't know how long I sat there. It was starting to get dark and I decided to see Helen, my friend from secondary school and someone I'd somehow managed to stay in touch with. She would instinctively know when to talk and when to leave me alone with my thoughts. To any casual observer, I was still in shock, but I could not stand to sit for too long and dwell on what had happened. I needed company and I needed distraction because I was still so scared.

Helen took me out. I would smoke to try and help me

think of something else; I was happy to be in bars or pubs as they were so loud and busy. But then the most extraordinary thing started to happen. Boys, men some of them, would come up to me and ask: 'Are you Natalia?' I'd hesitate but then they'd say something along the lines of: 'I've just come out of Lincoln prison and I've got a message from your dad.' The messages would be that he loved me or that he hoped I was OK, or to please call him soon. It was shocking. They were lads who looked as you'd expect – pretty rough, pretty scary some of them, and every one of them would say something about my dad being a 'top bloke'. He was known as 'granddad' and had quickly gained a reputation as someone who'd help read or write letters, as quite a few of the inmates were semi-literate and he was someone they'd turn to for advice.

I could hardly believe it: Dad had failed to be the voice of comfort and reason when we were growing up, and yet here he was, the father figure to all those petty criminals. It became a regular event, bumping into boys just released, acting like messengers. It reminded me how charming Dad could be, how quickly he would be able to attract people and how they'd be drawn to talking to him. One of them told me that the governor of the prison was Italian and that he'd call my dad into his office where they'd drink espresso and talk in Italian. I could barely believe it; I didn't know what to feel. This was too much. He'd been at 'death's door' from starvation and now he was acting as a prison counsellor. I wrote another letter, telling him not to forget what he had destroyed. I did not want him to enjoy solace and feel that everything would be fine; it wasn't.

You can't just walk in and visit during 'visiting hours' in prison: you have to wait to be sent a Visitor Order, which is a signed slip from the prisoner vetted through the prison staff. My slip arrived, and the idea that Dad was setting up a cosy environment at prison, charming those around him into thinking that he was a 'top bloke', still angered me. I was ready to confront him but when I saw him, he was far from relaxed – he was very agitated. He had been working on a letter that he'd addressed to the Queen and to Tony Blair. He gave me a copy of it. It was incredibly long, about 37 typed pages, and he talked in a way that I could not follow. He talked excitedly about 'sacred secrets', he said that he had been sent to 'reveal the Sacred Secrets of the Kingdom of God' and to sound the 'Horn of Alarm'; he also stood up and 'blessed' me telling me that he had forged a 'hedge of protection' around me, to keep me safe from Satan.

I was used to Dad talking at length and knowledgeably about the Bible. He studied it all the time and would talk in depth about the morals the stories held, but this was new. He was almost feverish as he told me that he was the Suffering Servant, the 'little one' of the Almighty God and his beloved Son. I was speechless. Then he read a passage from the letter that made my blood run cold:

I broke British Law once, and my Beloved wife broke God's Laws many times, and the Almighty God to save her Life sat in Judgement and with an Iron fist we Judged her and to save her Life, I had to apply his Judgement.

I stayed as calm as possible and told him that it was *his* judgement, not God's. But he was beyond me, beyond any of us. 'The British Judicial system is only equipped to deal with liars but when they are put in front of the truth, the Spiritual Truth, they stumble and because they do not understand, they persecute anyone who stands firm in the Truth,' he said.

I wish you could have heard his voice. Part of you listens, and knows that these are the words of a deluded old man, and yet if you sit in front of him, you find that you are pulled along by his logic until the reality of what his 'judgement' led to hits you like a fresh blow. He had convinced himself that what he had done, murdering the one woman he ever loved, was an act of love. Now, he wanted to convince everyone else. Yet the strain told. His letter was a bizarre combination of mathematical codes and scripture, a plea that 'the best mathematicians and computer programmers' help him to unravel the code.

I had no doubt now that Dad believed what he was saying. I asked him about Mum and told him how I felt, that I hated him for what he had done and again, he'd sob, saying, 'I'm so sorry, Natalia, I'm so sorry.' We'd both be in tears, but we were not consoling each other. He was as lost as I was but I knew his mind was unravelling in a very different way to mine. I was suffering with grief while he was lost to madness.

Any doubts I may have had were dismissed once I read and re-read his letter. Try as I might, I could not understand it. There was a lot of stuff about numbers, about Dad as a 'hidden watchman', persecuted by humankind. Of course, as anyone who came to speak to Bruno soon realised, if you disagreed with him, it was because you were one of the persecutors, one of the 'blind', resisting 'God's' message. It was the perfect delusion. Health professionals, lawyers, police, his family: we were all persecuting him. By challenging his view, we only added to his conviction.

He took lots of numbers from the Book of Daniel, or as he phrased it: TIME OF THE END. Daniel 10:2 = 3 Weeks = 21 Days + 7x7x7. It went on for page after page, in sequences I could not work out. The more I read, the more I realised that Dad had sealed himself off in this odd number-driven world of secrets and revelation. It was horrible. When my eyes scanned the pages again, I came across instructions like 'Analyse Please!!!!!!!'

It was macabre. My dad had not just joined the ranks of men who kill their wives – he had joined the list of people who send deranged letters to the authorities. His only apology to them was about his use of English, as he worried about his grammar. I knew that he had lost his mind and feared what he would attempt next.

His letter ended with more warnings about Satan being bound on Earth for a thousand years, until 2997. That of course meant he was heading for domination over earth now, the year then being 1997. Just as I was switching off, I read the last chilling sentence:

Satan knows in advance that the time to be loose is near, and he will prepare himself to destroy as many people as possible of Humankind. This is the way he thinks: 'If I can't be king over you, nobody else will be. And if I have to die, many of you will die with me.'

I read it again: 'If I can't be king over you, nobody else will be...' — that was how Dad had always behaved towards Mum. I felt at this moment that without him realising it, Dad had said more about his own state of mind than anything in the Bible. That was the true 'revelation', and despite all his contortions and justifications about acting as God's 'Iron fist', he had behaved like the avenging Satan he was desperate to warn humankind about.

Years later, I read that the scientist Isaac Newton had predicted the end of time as 2060 or some point after that. But when I saw that he based his predictions on calculations made in the Book of Daniel, my heart nearly stopped. Newton had written about the end of days, days that would see 'the ruin of the wicked nations, the end of weeping and of all troubles, the return of the Jews from captivity and their setting up a flourishing and everlasting Kingdom'. Apocalyptic visions and predictions are as old as time, but they still have the power to make me feel ill at ease. Dad was intelligent; he had a way of giving weight to even the strangest of ideas. I'm sure he would have loved to learn that Isaac Newton had studied the Book of Daniel as he had, even if their dates didn't agree.

Now I read about 'end times' and I feel unsettled, pushing anything I hear or see away, not wanting to dwell on it. Dad never told me a precise date but he did say that I might still be alive to see it. Although these were the words of a man lost in delusion, it is still chilling. Listening to Dad added massively to my sense of fear and exhaustion. I was exhausted not because I believed him, but because no matter how many times I tried to piece together what I'd been told and what I knew, including Dad's letters, I could not make sense of what had happened. I was fearful as I knew the family had been ripped apart forever and that the survivors, we four children, did not have enough common ground, love or understanding to stop our downward spiral.

I moved between states of hopelessness, anger and numbness. Grief is a strange thing – you can't shortchange it. The charge is high, just to grind through each day. Hearing that 'time heals' is a mockery as no one outside your grief understands what it means to get through an hour. And you are being asked to imagine years. To have lost Mum, say, to a heart attack, would have been terribly sad and the feeling of loss would have been sharp. But to know that your own father took her life – that he picked up a kitchen knife and deliberately made her suffer until she could no longer fight – pushes you into a mental hell that nothing can equip you for.

Time does not help as time demands that you imagine what she went through. What did she feel? Did she try to run? Was it quick or did she wait and wait for it to end? What was the last thing she saw? Was it my father, with a knife above his head? There are no short cuts when you have to leave behind horror; you see it frame by frame. It's replayed to you – your own mind as torturer.

There was a huge amount of anger, but it was massively misplaced because I grew angry with Mum. Why did she go there? Why, if she felt she was in any danger? Why would she allow him to do that and let him take her away from us? Without realising it, I was playing out age-old anger against my mum, once again blaming her, believing her weak in the face of Dad's rage.

Then at other times, I'd be forgetful and I would see something or hear something and happily think, Oh, I must tell Mum. I'd then be floored by loss again, yet still unable to really believe we were without her and that we'd always be without her.

The funeral was fast approaching and causing further friction. Long before Mum's death, Daiana and her husband had booked a weekend away in Paris; it fell just before the funeral. We all urged her to go: she looked shattered and it was clear that her relationship was suffering under the strain too. She had made all the arrangements for the funeral so it made sense for her to go, to try to find space away from us all and to grieve. But while she was away, one of the Jehovah's Witnesses came and visited Emmanuele. He looked at the plans for the service, including poetry that Daniel and I would read, and suggested that he re-write the service. Emmanuele agreed.

It was a catastrophe. No one else was told until the morning of the funeral. It turned into a Jehovah's service, something that still makes me angry to this day. It had nothing to do with Mum. We were shut out of our own mother's funeral. We were distraught, not least Daiana, who had returned to see all her plans ruined. She had tried her best to arrange a service that honoured Mum, but we felt it had been changed beyond all recognition.

So many people turned out to the service and the church was packed, which made the event all the harder to bear. I don't think Elva ever knew how much she was loved, nor how well thought of she was by those she'd met. Her kindness had shone through no matter how much Dad tried to restrict her. But the final insult for Daiana was yet to come. A bouquet had been collected in my name, but when it arrived I saw it was a floral arrangement that spelled out 7x7x7. I could not believe my eyes. Daiana went ballistic, 'That's not from you, Natalia. That's *him*! How could you do this?' I was horrified, but like the kid I had once been and still was when pressured, I thought I could lie my way out of her anger. 'No it isn't, it's mine,' I said, but even as I said it, I felt I had done the wrong thing.

It was too much. The press were hiding in the bushes even though we had specifically asked that they stay away. What should have been our chance to come together and honour our mother descended into farce and raw anger. There were members of Mum's family there and no one would speak to me. Mum's wake was being held at my Auntie Jean's house but there was no way I could walk through that door, the bad daughter, who even today was siding with her father. I wasn't, of course, but I did not have the strength to defend myself. I told Daiana that I wouldn't go and felt that once again, I was letting her down.

It was such a terrible day. I had nowhere to turn, so I asked Helen and some friends if they would come to the pub with me. I sat and raised a glass in Mum's honour – I never drink, but I wanted to mark the moment in some way. My mind kept turning back to an hour earlier when we had watched Mum's coffin slide forwards and the curtain shut behind her. That was the worst moment. I had visited her every day, sat with her and talked to her. The day before the funeral, I was told the coffin could no longer stay open as her body was deteriorating.

But now she had finally been taken from me and I was heartbroken. She had been taken. Never again hear would I her voice or look into her green eyes as she smiled and told me not to worry so much. The weight of loneliness I felt was too much to bear. Crying gave no relief, but I sat with my friends and the tears came. There was no one to save me now. I was falling, falling and there would be no phone call from Mum to say, 'Natalia, just come home.'

CHAPTER NINE

A SECRET REVEALED

And so I kept visiting Dad. I know there will be people who will never understand why but for me it was a way to keep Mum alive. Dad would talk about her, would cry and tell me stories that I loved to hear, old family favourites about when we were small and about Mum's funny ways, and I started to see a side of him that I'd never seen before. Now that he had poured out all his religious justifications, he seemed calmer and less ready to boil into anger, and somehow, far more thoughtful and subdued.

I know how that must sound. How can a murderer also be a kind and gentle man? I can only tell you what I saw and what I found. He was a man transformed by his sin; the old Bruno had gone and I was entering waters I did not understand, but I sensed that I was faced with a man who was so very different from the one I grew up with. I don't deny that part of me must have wanted to find that there was a man I could connect with, to try and understand. There must have been something in me that needed to believe that he was more than a monster.

During that same period, I visited Mum's grave. The headstone wasn't yet ready and so I'd lie on the grass next to the number put there by the council, and talk to her. My flatmate would worry about where I was, as I'd be missing for hours. Sometimes, I would just walk on the beach, where Mum used to love to walk, but I could be gone for four or five hours. After one episode, I could see how concerned he was, so I told him that the first place he should check was Mum's grave, and that's where he'd usually find me. It was coming up to a month since she had died. I was in limbo, not knowing where to turn. I had no money either and the plans I had to work alongside Mum had vanished along with everything else. The rent was due on the flat at Victoria Mills and I didn't know how I was going to pay it. My flatmate was out of work too and so it seemed that we'd have to move out. But where could I go? Back to Helen's, certainly not; to Daiana's – I wasn't sure. I spoke to Dad on the phone and he said, 'Why don't you move back into the house?' At first I was confused by what he meant; surely not the house in Old Crosby? But it was what he thought. I said no, as it didn't feel right but within a few days, I had changed my mind.

I'm not going to pretend that moving back into the family house, the house where my mum's life was taken, could be thought of as a sane move. It wasn't. But I had so lost my bearings that it made sense to me: I would go back home. There are people who would recoil in horror at the thought of moving back but I didn't believe that Mum was there. I was convinced that she was in Victoria Mills. I had fallen so far that being among Mum and Dad's stuff didn't worry me any more – in fact it brought me a certain comfort; it was familiar ground. My flatmate and I moved in. Looking back, I think it must have been the last straw for people who had read about the Aggiano family. What kind of daughter would move into the house where her mum was murdered? Part of me was shut down from grief and from a deeper damage; this house had been a battleground yet I was choosing to go back in. But I simply didn't know how to move on or move away. All I had was my instincts, usually wrong, and usually why I'd end up putting my hands in fire – finding out the hard way.

The police had not let us have access to the property for the first few weeks but now I was told that I could go in. They had removed the carpet in the back room and the fireplace. It dawned on me that it was because they proved how Mum had died; that they must have been blood-soaked. I wanted Dad to tell me precisely what had happened. Standing in the room made the event seems less, not more real. I needed to know the truth and so I visited Bruno.

'Tell me what happened; tell me exactly how Mum died,' I asked him.

He began to cry again but I sat silently until he was ready to talk. He started, 'Once Daniel went out to play and Emmanuele had left, I went in to the kitchen and locked the back door. The front was already locked.

'I knew what I had to do to save your mother. I loved her

149

so much, I did not want her soul to be condemned, so I knew that I must act. Jesus had appeared to me. I recognised him as he has appeared to me seven times before – I told you. I gave her a final warning and asked her to come back to me, but she said no. I went into the kitchen and I picked up the axe I use for cutting wood that I had hidden there. Your mum was sitting on the sofa, near the fireplace, with her back to me. I walked into the room and I struck her with the axe. She tried to stand up. She cried out, so I struck her again.

'The axe was not sharp enough, it was not working. I ran back into the kitchen and picked up the knives. The first blade was too long and bent when I struck your mother. I got another knife, a shorter one, and it bent too but only a little. She tried to get up, but fell forward on her knees, calling out. I don't remember stabbing her after that; it is a blank. I do remember the last thing she said, she said: "Now everyone will know you are a murderer." She was silent, then lying facing down.

'I sat with her. I turned her towards me and hugged her, caressing her. I told her I loved her and then I called work, Daiana and the police. It was over.'

I sat without moving. I had asked to know but I couldn't take in all he had said. It still seemed absurd; it could not have happened. 'Now everyone will know you are a murderer' – why had she said that? Did she think it would stop him, the shame of it? Or did she know that he had been killing her, killing us all by degrees all those years, and that now, finally, everyone would know about the brutality behind his careful public face? Why did she go to him? I was reeling, but I did not want to show Dad any more of how I felt. I needed to get away, to get back to the house where it had happened and to try and piece it all together again.

How is it possible to live with someone, to know them intimately, even their darkest nature and yet leave yourself so exposed? That went for both Mum and me. We knew Dad. We had both seen and suffered different aspects of his rage; neither of us were taken in by his intelligence or his charm. We knew what he was capable of. 'Natalia, he will kill me if he sees me again', she had said. 'He has stabbed her, hasn't he?' I had asked the police. We both knew. I had even gone as far as to work out what method, what weapon he'd used. And yet on that last day, in that final hour, our judgement had deserted us both. Both of us had looked into his dark heart and had turned away, thinking that that last brutal act was beyond him, after all. But all it had been was beyond our imagination. We had scared ourselves with the idea, but in the end we had not believed it. Like children trying to wish away the monster under the bed, holding onto the fact that the monster had not got us yet. Perhaps he doesn't exist after all, we hoped.

Dad wrote of himself as the 'little one', but he had never been more wrong. The little one was Mum, with her pure heart and honest hope that all would be well; that the monster wouldn't strike. And what would have destroyed her was not the realisation that she was wrong to trust Dad in those last few minutes but the horrific moment when she knew that her children would be left behind – especially Daniel – that would have crushed her and caused her far more pain than Dad's fury.

I had been truly burned this time. I sank to my knees because I knew that my pact with Dad would yield yet more secrets, perhaps more than I could bear. Yet the truth, at least, is a white heat – it is intense, even if it offers no guarantee that you will survive. But lies burn with a different heat and destroy less cleanly; something I was soon to find out for myself.

Many of the neighbours had started to gossip about the house and it did not take long for my presence to take a new and malicious turn. I've little doubt that my mum's old friends and neighbours had a part to play, perhaps now enjoying their outrage, as Daiana was called with some spectacular tales. Perhaps if they had not been so lurid they could have caused more damage, but even as they were, they were enough to deepen the rift with my sister and have a terrible effect on my brother-in-law's actions.

Daiana had been told that I was 'entertaining men', and that any number were to be seen traipsing in and out of the house. I named them for Daiana, most of them gay friends that she knew and friends of my flatmate. But the implication that I was a prostitute was only the start. Next came claims that I had painted the walls red and was charging people £10 to come in and see where the murder had taken place. I barely knew what to say to this. I simply asked Daiana to come round and look for herself – it was ludicrous. She dismissed it, but it was clear that my decision to live in the old house was only bringing out the worst in people.

Perhaps the notoriety of the house and the general feeling that I was no good gave people license to say, and now do, as they pleased. I had gone out to buy some food when I returned to find the house had been broken into. There was no damage and nothing of value had been taken; It was more disturbing than that. Photographs had been taken —mementoes, macabre souvenirs from the house of horror. And it wasn't to be the only time. Over the next few months, there were other break-ins, again, just to take trivial stuff. Once my flatmate came home to see young blokes running out of the front door – we always came in from the back. It made me realise that the house was being watched. But on the last occasion, I was sleeping upstairs alone and came down in the morning to see that there had been another break-in. It was too much.

When my flatmate's car was stolen, I knew we were thought of as fair prey and that we would have to leave. At the same time, a letter arrived from my sister's solicitors to say that she and her husband were applying for custody of Daniel and that they did not want me to have access to him any more. In fairness to my sister, she did not try to block me seeing Daniel, and they lived close by, so I saw a lot of him. But it was different if her husband was around. If he saw me in the street and he was with Daniel, he would quickly walk past, telling him not to talk to me.

In his eyes I was an unreliable, jobless dope addict and unfit to spend time with Daniel. What they didn't know was that Daniel would call on me quite a lot, saying he was going out to see friends, but walking around the corner to see me. He made me promise not to tell Daiana as there was no doubt that she'd be horrified to know that he had spent time in the house where his mother had been murdered. But he'd come and sit with me and ask me questions, often about how Dad was. I would say little, just that he was OK, that we were waiting for his trial and that I would help him see Dad if he chose.

My view was that if he was angry with Dad, if he hated him, if he hated him, he had every right to tell him to his face. Dad would tell me that he loved Daniel and that he missed him, but it was easy for him to sentimentalise – he didn't have to look into the eyes of his 9-year-old and know that his actions had left him an orphan. If Daniel wanted to vent his rage and tell him how he'd ruined his life, I thought he should be allowed to do so. But Daniel said he did not want to see him. I'm glad I never pushed him. He was still a child and what would it have done to him? As it was, Daniel was to go through a lot of suffering, and his rage was to turn in on him, but none of us knew how to help him at that point. I loved him and the fact that my brother-in-law felt he knew best and that he wanted us kept apart tore into me.

In truth, I was messed up. I was using dope to numb what I felt more than I should have been. But asking Daniel to think of me as a bad person was the wrong thing to do. I felt for Daiana: her marriage was breaking apart under the strain and all she wanted to do was to protect Daniel, something we'd all failed to do so far. But I'd be damned if that meant I had to cease contact and so I went to a solicitor myself. My GP had diagnosed that I had depression, which meant that I was on incapacity benefit in the months after Mum's death. That meant that when I consulted a solicitor, it was free. My sister had to pay for each letter and meeting. I said to her that we should just sort it out and stop wasting money.

I could seem so tough, so belligerent but behind that front I was still a scared little girl and I was struggling to keep myself from falling apart. Having something to fight about was familiar ground and I could still whip myself up into a righteous temper when I thought about my brother-in-law. He'd never liked me, but then I'd never liked him and so it was the perfect way for me to vent my frustration. I didn't care what he thought about me: he could go to hell as far as I cared.

I didn't know what I could do next, other than move out of the house. I had been there about six months and still there was no sign of Dad's case coming to trial. I was drifting, but my emotional health was about to take a turn for the worse. I was about to walk back into the life of a girl I had known at primary school, and we were about to embark on a new journey of destruction, both of us damaged and so very wrong for each other. I'll call her Jess.

Jess walked past the house and saw me hanging out some washing, and she seemed so concerned about me. She said that when she had heard about Mum, she had run to the house but the police had stopped her from coming inside. Jess told them that she was an old friend of mine and needed to know if I was OK, but they would not tell her how to find me. Hearing her say all those things comforted me. So many people were avoiding me and even those that weren't, didn't dare mention Mum. Jess just seemed to want to know if I was OK.

A few days later, we met up for a drink. I just had an orange juice, but Jess drank and drank. This was to set the pattern for us for the next few years. I've never really liked alcohol, but Jess had a thirst for it. I realised that despite her loud and confident behaviour, she was far from OK. She never knew her father and her strict and domineering mother had been pressurising her to agree to an arranged married. She disapproved of her daughter's behaviour, dressing improperly, drinking and staying out, and Jess was finding her home life impossible. She was very tough, very quick to lose her temper and kick off if she thought someone was being disrespectful in pubs and clubs but behind closed doors, she was desperately unhappy. We gravitated to each other, each sympathetic to the other's misery and decided that we were sisters in all life had to throw at us.

And Jess could be great fun – she was always cracking jokes and happy to stir up a bit of excitement or adventure. She was restless and complained about life in Scunthorpe; it was just too boring and there had to be more out there. We made a vow to each other to run away. Jess said, 'I'll live on the streets before I ever agree to get married.' I didn't tell her anything about the realities of life on the streets, I just liked to hear how determined she was not to let anyone push her around.

Despite all we had in common, we were very different in temperament. Even though I was the source of most of the rows between my family, beyond that I hated conflict. I would always back down and walk away, no matter what anyone said. It wasn't the case with Jess. She once head-butted a girl in a pub because she'd made a mean comment to me about Mum. When she was pulled off the girl, she was screaming, 'No one says anything like that to my sister, no one!' It quickly became clear that Jess was to be avoided. She was like a bodyguard to me when we went out, just waiting to lose it over the mildest provocation.

Other friends took me aside and tried to warn me that this new friendship was a bad idea, but I wouldn't listen. I just said that she did what she did because she cared about me and was looking out for me. When people said she was bad news, I pushed it aside. It never dawned on me that I was placing someone with a violent and possessive temper back in the centre of my life. I just didn't see it – I saw someone who cared. We quickly became inseparable. She would drive me to see Dad and would sit outside the prison waiting for me. I didn't drive, and so found that I was more and more reliant on her and soon she was organising exactly what we would do and on what day – if Jess said 'jump', I would say 'how high?'

Prison scared me and it helped to have Jess travel there with me. Once you enter the prison, you have your possessions taken away, you are searched and reminded of the dos and don'ts. I was visiting Dad about once a month and no matter how off-putting it was, I had a need to see him and to talk about Mum. We'd both sit there sobbing but the prison staff kept their distance. Dad would talk in Italian and I would listen, tears running down my face. He told me how hard Mum saved for my roller blades and how he wasn't sure who was the happiest that morning, Mum or me, once I'd opened the box and realised what they were.

He told me how happy she was when I was born, her 'little doll'; how she had waited and waited for her next child to arrive and how happy she was when I came into the world. I needed to hear about Mum; I needed to hear about when she was happy and when everything was OK, and how I had made her happy. All the time, it was her killer offering me these memories and these comforts. I remember sobbing to Daiana on the phone and her saying, 'Don't see him, Natalia. He's messing with your mind.' Perhaps he was; perhaps by feeding me these memories he was making sure that I would always go back for more. But no matter how twisted his love for her was, it was love. He was in as much pain as I was and reliving memories of Elva cost him dearly. Look what he had destroyed. I never offered him forgiveness for what he had done but slowly we were finding a new way to be together, this father and daughter, and it was painful but increasingly important to me. I could not turn away from it or pretend that I did not want to listen to him.

Other than Jess, the only encouragement I got for seeing Dad came from his family. They had written and said what a good girl I was for staying loyal to Bruno and doing my duty as a daughter. This made me feel worse, not better. In their eyes, God approved of what I was doing. In my eyes, there was no God – at least, not a God who would demand my mum's life.

The only good news I'd had was that Daiana had dropped the court case about access to Daniel. The terrible thing was that her marriage was over and she was seeking a divorce. It seemed as if the fall-out from Dad's actions just kept coming. In the middle of all this chaos, I would see Dad. The one part of my life that I suppose from the outside should have sent my emotions into a tailspin was becoming the time when I found a little more calm. I could now tell my dad anything. I warned him that he could not dictate to me or forbid me to do things as he had when I was young and his reaction surprised me. He stared at me intently and said, 'Natalia, I will tell you what I think, what I believe truthfully, but you are my baby girl and I will not be angry with you.'

Baby girl! Here was the dad that this baby girl had never known. This was new territory. Why did Dad saying it matter so much? I had never been his baby girl; I had never been the one who had shown him much promise or affection or dutiful obedience. But rather than extinguishing the love I should have felt for him, I was like a fire starved of oxygen. And his attention was like breath on embers, but unstable, like combustion. Never has the phrase 'playing with fire' meant so much, yet this was just the beginning of a new set of revelations.

I felt raw. I needed to be honest about my life, about all the mistakes I was making. I told Dad about my drug-taking and as he sat and held my hand, without judging me, only feeling my pain, I knew that I could tell him more, tell him everything. I told him about being raped at the canal. I could see the pain that it caused him, the idea that his baby girl should have suffered in this way.

'If only you had told your mother,' he said. And then came the bombshell: 'You know, Natalia, when I met your mother, she was so very sad too. She had made many mistakes.' I asked him what he meant. Elva was a young teenager – what mistakes could she have made?

He was quiet for a moment and then said, 'When I first heard about your mother, it was from another Italian man. He said that she would go with men into the woods and she'd let them have sex with her.' He stopped, as if sensing that my mind was in collision at this point: he can't have meant Mum.

He continued: 'She was confused. She would offer herself to men but I could see that she knew what she was doing wasn't right, that it was making her unhappy.'

'Dad, what are you talking about?'

'What she did was sinful. But a terrible thing had happened to her, Natalia.'

'*What* terrible thing?' I asked. I was surprised at how steady my voice was. It sounded distant to me, but my heart was thudding in my chest from dread and confusion.

'She had been raped as a child – a man known to her family. She was only 8 years old. She told her mother but her mother did not believe her. It happened more than once.'

My head was spinning. My knuckles were white as I clutched the edges of the table. This could not be right, this could not have happened. I stared at Dad and he looked back at me with concern.

'Are you OK, Natalia?'

I shook my head.

'Why didn't she tell me?' I asked.

'I don't know,' he said. 'I think it was too hard for her. All her life, I told her that I would look after her, that what happened was a sin but that she could absolve that sin by becoming a dutiful wife and a good mother; that God would see and understand.'

Why didn't she tell me, why didn't I know? All that time, when she'd heard me talk about the men I was sleeping with, all the mistakes I was making – why didn't she reach out and say, stop Natalia, I know what pain you are in? But I hadn't told her about the night at the canal. I was too ashamed and perhaps shame was what had stopped her too. It had prevented her from pushing away the lies and the deceit, and helped her to say that Dad was the only man she'd ever know, that she was ignorant about sex and men.

But she wasn't ignorant; she knew too much. By 8 she knew too much and when she met Dad at 17, she knew too much. She had rebelled against her father, the strict rule follower who had failed to protect or believe her, so when a handsome Italian walked into her life and told her that he knew the way to make it all go away, she placed herself in his hands. I think that Dad truly wanted to help her but he also believed that, as an 8-year-old, she was a sinner too, that the blame was in part hers. That was a terrible thing for him to have said. It was also an evil thought that took root in him, allowing him to harvest his many doubts over Elva's obedience and purity thereafter. He had created a lie about Mum's life too, warning her that if her children ever knew about her early life of drinking and promiscuity, they would disown her. This was another terrible hold he had had over her.

In his jealous heart, did he believe that she would stray again, that the stain of sin could never be cleansed if he did not watch over her? Did Elva walk into that marriage believing this was her chance for redemption, never realising that only a vengeful and jealous God watched over her, and would never free her? Her jailer could find it in his heart to love her, but never to release her. And now he sat there, his own freedom stripped from him, labelled a killer. Is that what Mum meant? Did she see this when she said with her dying words: 'Now everyone will know that you are a murderer.'

I could not process everything Dad had told me; I was unable to contain all I heard. I needed to speak to Daiana. Did she know? I tried to compose myself when I got home, in an effort to call her. She said that yes, Mum had written to her and told her what had happened shortly after moving to Victoria Mills. I slumped to the floor, nothing stopping the tears now. That young girl, so damaged, and what had I done to help her? Nothing. Now she'd never know how much I loved her and how sorry I was for all she had been through.

When Daiana spoke to me, she remained calm. She had to; she could not afford to collapse into grief again. She had Daniel to cope with, a full-time job to hold down and a mortgage to pay. No wonder she looked at me with dismay. I was crashing through so many emotional barriers; in her eyes I was out of control. And now I was pushing harder, finding out about Mum and causing yet more anguish for myself and everyone around me.

Who was the man who raped Mum? I was half-crazed with the thought that it had happened. Why didn't her own mother protect her or believe her? How could any man destroy a child in that way? What I felt for Mum collided into all I had felt that night at the canal: utter hopelessness and shame, the stain it leaves. Looking in the mirror and knowing you are not that person any more, that all has changed. The world is not safe, you are not innocent, you will have to carry the ruin and the pain. No one will come to your aid: you did not matter enough.

Is this what I had wanted when I asked Dad for his honesty? If I could gather the pieces of myself again, history forever changed, would it be worth it? What was I left with? Fear, horror, hopelessness. I feared making the same mistakes Mum had made; I feared the life I still had to live.

Amid this turmoil, I knew Dad's trial was imminent. How would I cope with the trial, and my knowledge that Mum and I shared a terrible secret? Then the news came that the trial date was set for the end of March, in Lincoln. It was coming up to a year since Mum had died. Jess said that she would drive me to the court and we set off. Again, I felt that time was standing still. To add to the stress, the press were waiting. I was literally chased down the street until I found PC Broughton. I trusted him, and I told him what was happening. He stood between the press and me, but I doubted that I would be able to cope with it day after day.

Talking to the press was a risk. At first, after Mum's death, I thought that the best thing was to be honest and give short statements. But seeing the words in print, often in a new context, made me realise that the press were interested in a story, not the truth. The truth is a mess anyway and what they needed was a snappy sentence or headline to meet the story they were planning. And look how I could be represented – the daughter who stood by her father, her mother's killer. The truth was far more complex, but that wouldn't be a story that was going to make the news. Far better to chase me down and get me to say, 'I stand by my dad.' It would make good copy, get people shaking their heads over their cornflakes... But I don't think the press are monsters; they know what their readers want to see and I've been on both sides of the divide. I've read horrible stories, too, taken in the easy first paragraph and turned the page, giving it no more thought. The only thing that's different now is that when I read those things, I know I'm not getting the whole story, and that I shouldn't expect to in a paper or a magazine.

I was at the court, but sick with nerves. I was waiting to see Dad but when he was finally called up from the cells, the trial was delayed again because one of the jury members felt ill. The jury was dismissed but Dad was left sitting there for a few minutes while the prison staff organised his walk back down to the cells. He had the chance to call me over. The court was emptying, so I made my way over to him. He started crying – he looked so much older, so much smaller than I remembered – and he said, 'Natalia, I could not call you. The phone was cut off and did not know if I would see you again.'

I started crying too. The phone had been cut off as I hadn't been able to pay the bill and I hadn't realised that Dad had tried to call.

At that moment I felt terrible, and said, 'Dad, I'm so sorry, I am. Of course you will see me again.'

I gave him a hug and then he froze and said, 'Look behind you.'

I turned around and there was Aunty Jean, sitting in one of the rows glaring at us. I was horrified. What must I have looked like, comforting her sister's killer? She gave me the blackest look and I can't say I blame her. I just froze. My instinct had been to hug Dad. I had felt bad for not seeing him but in Aunty Jean's eyes, I was confirming everything she'd heard about me. I had got it all wrong yet again.

Dad was led out of the court room and soon afterwards, his solicitor approached me. He looked concerned and said that he was going to take me down to the cells to see Dad and that something had happened. I couldn't think what it could be – perhaps he was ill? But as I got nearer I could see that he was shaking and was in pain. I asked him what had happened. He told me that he had wanted to bring his bible along to the court, as usual, but that morning, it had been left behind. He had wanted to return to his cell for it, but the prison staff needed to get him into the van and on their way. He had resisted and it had all kicked off.

He lifted up his shirt to show me and I was shocked. Along his ribs and back was swelling and bruising. It upset me because Dad was clearly not well and relied on his bible. I was shocked to see so many bruises on an old man. I got up and wanted to complain, but the solicitor said that it was being dealt with through the proper channels. As it turned out, it was, although I don't know if anyone was disciplined. But from then on, the Governor made it clear that Dad was to be given his bible before he left the prison.

Dad's legal team had had him assessed by psychiatrists. I think the prosecution may have done so as well, as he had seen several specialists. His solicitor told me that they were looking at a plea of manslaughter on the grounds of diminished responsibility. Their argument was that the balance of Dad's mind had been disturbed when he decided to kill Mum. The problem was that manslaughter usually means an unplanned murder – typically, you just snap and lash out and it ends in a death. Clearly, Dad had planned the event, which should mean it was murder. The fact that he had got Mum to the house, sent his sons away, locked the doors and hidden a murder weapon – the axe – meant that it was a premeditated act.

I know that's what a lot of my family will always believe; and also that all his protestations that God told him to do it had been an act, carried out in the hope that he'd get a reduced sentence. If it was an act, he'd given a sterling performance in the months before the trial. He had written many letters based on quotes and codes in the bible and had battled with the prison psychiatrists. He had warned them that the court was equipped only for liars, not the Truth and that he was a servant of God.

This was what he wrote: 'How can he be the servant of God? He is guilty of murdering his wife. They will see only the outside appearance, that is the flesh. The Truth, the Spiritual Truth, is hidden from them. When the Almighty God condemned the human generation at the time of the Flood, was he guilty of murder?

'When he condemned Sodom and Gomorrah, was he guilty of murder? When he condemns anyone, is He a murderer? And the ones who executed his judgement, are they guilty of murder? Do not think that I am in favour of murder, it is an abomination. To do the will of Almighty

God, the Ancient of Days, is a Blessing. Even if this brings persecution, no matter how hard, my reward is waiting for me in the Resurrection in the Kingdom of God.'

I could see how it made him look. I think it was truly what he believed but it dawned on me that he looked insane and that the outcome would not be prison but a mental institution. I even told him so and warned him that any more religious ravings could mean that he was heading for the 'loony bin'. He told me that I had watched too many movies. He was calm and I really think that he believed the court would have some sort of 'revelation', that they would suddenly see he was powerless to act against 'God's judgement'. He was beyond calm but believed every word of what he said.

The frightening thing is that in making statements about 'God's will', Bruno was far from alone. It isn't what drives every husband who kills his wife but all to often it appears as a justification. And beyond murder, there are acts of coercion women are asked to put up with every day in 'God's' name. Men everywhere believe they are carrying out 'God's will' when they punish unruly wives or daughters. In some countries, a woman can be stoned to death or murdered by their families for committing 'adultery' or 'bringing shame' on the family, and far from being punished, they are backed by 'God's law'. Even girls born here have been punished for not agreeing to arranged marriages, or pay the ultimate price as victims of 'honour killings'. It makes me shudder to think that in another culture, Dad may well not have been punished for taking his wife's life.

As it stood, in a British court, his actions were those of a madman. In his mind, he wasn't mad, and he could talk in a way that made him sound crazy to the jurors, yet in his mind, he was perfectly logical and composed. All I knew for certain was that he had done a terrible thing and should be punished. But what would life be like in a mental institution? It filled me with more dread than prison. I had every kind of fear. This wasn't petty criminals and drug addicts; this was more the likes of the Yorkshire Ripper and the Moors Murderer Ian Brady. I felt sick thinking about what kind of institution held the criminally insane, yet Dad was oblivious and felt sure that if the court didn't listen to reason and realise that he was acting on God's behalf, they would convict him and send him back to Lincoln prison. He never wanted to be free – he wanted to be understood but there was little doubt that he felt sorry for his actions, even if he was 'forced' to kill. In his mind, it did not feel wrong to be made to pay for Elva's death. He wasn't interested in freedom and never once spoke about it. I think what he yearned for was understanding. He wanted people to accept that he had truly loved Mum and that he was powerless to act against the instruction to kill her.

I made it absolutely clear to him that no matter how it appeared that I 'stood by' him, I would never accept that he had done anything other than a terrible thing. He never attempted to change my mind; he never pleaded with me, only answered my questions as best he could. We'd never come to an understanding on the point where he picked up the knife. Those few moments would divide us forever. On that day, he stood on the side of the Devil, not the angels as far I would ever understand it.

I asked about the next day in court but was told that it was impossible to know if there would be any more adjournments. I could arrive to find that it was not in session that day, and as I didn't drive, Jess wasn't happy with the idea of turning up everyday for no reason. So I was completely taken by surprise when the very next day, Dad's trial reached a sudden conclusion.

Dad had entered a plea of not guilty to murder, yet during the trial, during a long monologue, he told the jury that he had decided to take Mum's life because he still loved her and was not prepared to see her spirit destroyed. The judge then directed the jury that there was no defence of 'necessity' under English law and that the only viable verdict now was 'guilty'.

A psychiatrist, Dr Earp, testified that Bruno was suffering from a delusional disorder, and so the Crown, which means the prosecution, announced that they accepted Dad's responsibility was 'diminished' during the time of the murder. That quickly wrapped up the trial as both sides now accepted that Mum's death was 'manslaughter'. The judge then thanked the jury and said that Bruno would go back to Lincoln where he would be assessed by yet more psychiatrists, only this time they would be from a top security hospital where he would be admitted for treatment.

Dad called to tell me of the decisions the judge took that day but seemed not to have taken on board the full impact of what it meant to be detained indefinitely at a hospital for the mentally ill. It hit me hard. Dad didn't realise what this meant. He was expecting to go back to Lincoln prison and on some level, he might have been happy there. He had a group of younger inmates that he would help with writing and reading letters; he had access to a computer and a printer so he could keep exploring his ideas about the End Days, and I think returning there would have suited him just fine.

Instead, within a month, he would be taken to Rampton, a high security hospital, and there would be no date set for his release. I know that some people think that a mental hospital is an easier option when it comes to serving a sentence. But in prison, you have a set term, and parole usually happens after about two-thirds of it has been served. That's not the case somewhere like Rampton, where you have to prove that you are mentally well again and that you no longer pose a threat to the community. This is far from straightforward and in fact it proved impossible for Dad. He would serve out the remainder of his days in secure hospitals, with no prospect of release. But all this lay ahead of us, and my feeling of dread at this point was based on ignorance. I had no idea what was to happen and in many ways, it was worse than I had imagined.

Rampton is the kind of building you would associate with a mental hospital. Although it was built in the early twentieth century, it has the kind of architecture that makes it look like a Victorian institution – it is built from red bricks and you feel apprehensive just looking at it. I had arrived by train, about a week after Dad had been sent there. I'd missed the connecting bus which took me to the hospital and the taxi fare cost me £15, almost wiping me out of cash. But I'd promised Dad I'd come and see him. I was anxious, but once I entered the reception area, I felt a little better. It was light and well decorated, and I started to push all the ideas I had about metal institutions, like patients being held down and electrocuted, aside. But the feeling that things would be OK didn't last. I was led through a metal detector, like the machines you have in airports, and down series of corridors, each locked behind me. They became dingier and dingier, and my heart sank: it was truly awful.

There are about 400 patients in Rampton, and around three-quarters of them are there because they have committed a very serious crime, many of the others because of metal and physical disabilities that mean they need 24-hour care. There is a huge number of staff, about 1,800 or so, but violence erupts every day and the carers regularly end up in the A&E department. The NHS Trust running Rampton have even been taken to court by the nursing staff over negligence because they have suffered injuries such as broken arms in their attempts to restrain violent patients.

This hospital is home to the 'Angel of Death', Beverley Allitt, the nurse who is serving 13 life sentences for killing four babies and attacking many others in her care. There are paedophiles and the seriously unbalanced. I remember one guy, good-looking and around 25 years old. He was leaning against the wall and then dropping himself to the floor, over and over again. I was told that he and his girlfriend had had a suicide pact but the pills they overdosed on killed her and he survived. I could feel sorry for him but other inmates were just terrifying. There was a man dubbed 'the vampire'. He'd killed his mum and dad, among others, and had a fetish for sucking the blood of his victims.

I realised immediately that was very different from life in prison. In Lincoln prison, you could visit and the staff would walk about at the back of the hall at a discreet distance. At Rampton, staff would sit in on the visit and even take notes. After the first few attempts to talk to me, Bruno started to talk to me in Italian. I could say hardly anything in reply but could follow a lot of what he was saying as he talked about Mum. What I didn't realise was that our conversations were taped anyway and later transcribed. The assessment of patients' mental state of mind is continuous, even if you are just watching TV or reading, and phone calls are listened in to. It's not an easy ride, and unlike prison, you are not left in your cell except for meals and exercise. You have to attend psychiatric sessions where you are probed about how you think and act. That and group sessions make for a fraught enough time – you are not allowed to forget why you are there and others' instability leaves you on high alert. And then there's the drug regime.

Within a few weeks of Dad's admittance to Rampton, I saw huge changes in him. He couldn't hold a conversation – he was vague, he would forget what he was talking about and looked disorientated; he also looked much older. This was a new shock to me as he'd always had facts and figures at his fingertips and would talk quickly and clearly on whatever topic you introduced. I had had a lifetime of hardly ever agreeing with him but this was new; he could not concentrate on what I was saying. He begged me to help him commit suicide: he wanted to die rather than stay at Rampton.

I spoke to the staff to try and find out what was happening but they said he was fine. To demonstrate my point, I stood in front of him and said, 'Dad, I'm a drug dealer.' He said nothing, just nodded, and so I went on: 'Dad, I'm a prostitute. I've been caught by the police', and he just nodded a little. He was clearly disinterested or unable to take in what I was saying and so I lost it entirely, screaming: 'What have you done to my dad? get him out of here!' Eventually, two male members of staff led me away. I was taken to see Dad's 'social worker', who tried to explain that Dad was given medication to stop him thinking too deeply about God and his voices. I was enraged, I pointed out that as he couldn't process anything, how did they even expect him to work out whether what he'd done was wrong? He was just a zombie rocking in a chair.

Dad's medication was not changed and although his mind seemed to adjust, his ability to recall dates and events, something he used to do effortlessly, was lost. Now I would have to prompt him and sometimes even that was not enough. The question I had to ask myself was why did it matter to me whether or not he was taking prescribed medication? I had to face up to the fact that I wanted him to be able to focus and talk to me. I needed his mix of memories about Mum and the chance it gave me to grieve but also his words of advice. Almost everything I told him about, and he warned me about, came to pass. He had a lightening quick mind and could tell when I was straying onto the wrong path with the wrong person. Now I would tell him things about my life before anyone else. I knew also that I didn't need to heed his advice, and that was important too. He did not judge me for my mistakes; that was the lesson he had learnt.

But there was a deeper truth at work too. It was because I loved and needed this new dad I had found. I had known what it meant to be fatherless and the need to be cared for had not left me – it had grown. I used to call him the Italian Papa, but now I used Dad, recognising that we were both in new territory. Being able to see him also gave me the hope that I could live without bitterness or hatred in my heart. Little did I know, I still had so far to go.

CHAPTER TEN

THE WRONG LIFE
TO LEAD

It was March 1999, two months after my twenty-first
Birthday and a year after the trial. My twenty-first should
have been the cause of a big celebration: it is often thought
of as a landmark, but I felt I had little to celebrate. I was
living in Hull with a dead-beat boyfriend, working in
McDonalds, still grieving for my mother, estranged from
my family, and now I found out that I was pregnant. Jess was
the first person I told.

The summer before, just after Dad's committal to
Rampton, Jess had said: 'We're moving to Hull.' I didn't
hesitate. I wanted out of Scunthorpe – my life there was
finished and I felt nothing but the oppressiveness of people
who knew all about me. The idea of running away to
somewhere I wasn't known was all I wanted. My one fear
was being away from Daniel but Jess said that she would
drive me back to see him as well as Dad.

So in June 1998, we set off for Hull and a flat that belonged to someone Jess knew. The flat was OK and I decided to start smoking less and to try and get work, either temping or back at McDonalds. Downstairs from the flat, there were two guys who knew Jess's friend and they soon became regular fixtures in our flat. I'll call them Sam and Shaun. Shaun was quieter, a genuinely nice bloke but not as confident as his friend Sam. Sam was a serous pot smoker, out of work and with no interest in finding any.

I liked Shaun a lot but didn't know how to tell him. However, Sam zeroed in on me and I was soon pushed along into starting a relationship with him. At first, he was very attentive, good company and clearly keen on me. He was pretty intense straightaway, telling me that he loved me and that we should be together. Within a couple of weeks, I was living with him. Jess didn't mind as it meant a ready supply of drugs and somewhere else to hang out. She was involved with more than dope but I turned a blind eye to it and was still trying to cut down on what I was smoking. Any drug use, even alcohol, means you seek out people who use as much or even more of the substance than you, as it normalises your behaviour and is yet another easy excuse to have another session. In all the time I spent with addicts, I came across few true friendships. These people would spend hours and hours in each other's company, talking endlessly, but in the main the relationship was with the drug and not each other.

You could waste your life this way, and people do. It's the perfect ritual and distraction – life happens elsewhere and you avoid the pain. It's all a delay though. And sooner or later, you find your demons have gone nowhere – they've just taken a backseat while you mess yourself up a little more. Sam had his reasons to anaesthetise. His dad had committed suicide when he was a young boy and his relationship with his mum was pretty messed up. She had other grown-up children too but Sam always behaved like a kid around her. I think she'd had enough of kids but that only made him more needy. Her own daughters had children of their own but she made it very clear that her home wasn't a dumping ground – they could do the child rearing: she wasn't going to shoulder the responsibility.

She could be hard-faced and pretty hard-hearted too. Whether that was just her way of getting through it all – maybe she was just worn out by life – or whether she truly didn't care, was never clear to me. Either way, the end result was the same: she spent much of her time on the verge of anger and I was scared of her. She disapproved of me, and of pretty much anyone in her son's life, seeing them as the source of the problems in Sam's life, and that was that.

Life with Sam was far from easy. He wasn't the laidback and chilled bloke he imagined he was as a smoker, far from – he had a terrible temper and would lose his head completely over the smallest thing. Smoking makes a lot of users paranoid and it took Sam very little to think that I was being 'out of order'. Maybe it was talking to one of my male friends, even if they were gay, it didn't matter to Sam. Whatever it was that day, he would pick a fight with me. By then, I'd stopped smoking completely and I was again working in McDonalds, so that made matters worse. We were completely out of synch. Dope heads exist in their own worlds anyway, and now I just seemed to exist on the outside, antagonising him. Not that he wanted me out of his life, far from it. He was incredibly possessive and spent more and more time monitoring 'my behaviour', waiting for me to trip up. When I did, perhaps by saying something flippant, like, 'Don't worry, I'm sure that washing up will sort itself out,' it was his excuse to lose himself in a righteous fury.

I wouldn't fight back; I just hid away waiting for it to be over. There was only one occasion when I snapped. He'd been on at me for hours and I was trying to take my make-up off, thinking that if I could just get into bed it would all go away, when he shoved me in the back, so I turned around and threw my plastic cleanser bottle at him. He stormed out and I thought no more of it until I heard that his mum was braying for my blood. He'd told her that I'd, 'thrown a bottle at his head', and she was on the war path. She stormed into the flat and moved Sam out, but within a few days, he was banging on the door begging me to get back together – and I stupidly let him back into my life.

I visited Dad and told him how unhappy I was. Over the months he had adjusted to his drugs regime and he could sit and focus on me, listening calmly. He told me to end the relationship, that Sam was not the man for me and that he did not have it in him to make me happy. Every word rang true. Dad would take the time to talk to me with sympathy and compassion, but this was the same advice as friends were giving me – no one liked the way Sam treated me, so why didn't I listen to what they said? Why did Dad saying it matter so much?

Shaun was by far a better listener and often we found ourselves talking into the night as Sam crashed out. Much later, Shaun told me that he had wished he could rescue me, and take me away from it all, but back then, we were both feeling helpless. My relationship with Sam grew to become ever more destructive. During one row, he pushed me backwards and I slipped, putting my hand out to stop my fall. My hand crashed down into a glass and it shattered, leaving me with cuts and glass embedded in my palm. The volume of blood shocked me; it was just running out, soaking through anything I wrapped around it. Sam was in a panic and it was clear that we'd have to go to A&E. He was crying and apologising, promising that it would never happen again. At the emergency room, I told them I had slipped and fallen. They took out what glass they could and I had seven stitches. Sam held me on the way home but I sensed that any effort I was trying to make to pull my life back together would fail if I stayed here with him.

On the day of my twenty-first birthday, Sam decided to throw a party. I don't remember much about the day – I think it was little more than an excuse to smoke and get ripped. It seemed extraordinary to me that we had stuck together for eight months but it said little except that all I could do with my life at this point was tread water. I was still so fragile, and being reminded that I would see 21 without my mum worsened my mood. Milestones make loss all the harder to bear. I did not enjoy the party and in the early hours of the morning, people began to drift away. That left Sam and me, and the atmosphere had an edge to it. Sam was a bit hyper and wanted us to have sex. I told him

I wasn't interested. He pulled at me and I told him to get off, but he wouldn't. Then I just switched off. In my head I retreated, I was numb and thought, let him get on with it.

The next morning, I went to work and I don't think Sam even gave it a thought. It is hard for me to come to terms with the fact that my boyfriend, someone I should have been able to trust and feel secure with, used me in this way. It disgusted me, the fact that he could even begin to imagine that it was OK to force himself on me. Although it was not as traumatic as the attack by the canal, I think it did irreparable damage to my relationships with men thereafter. The huge irony was that for the first time, I had begun to open up to Sam sexually. He had taken the time to make sure that I enjoyed sex, not just endured it. And so his betrayal was that much harder to cope with. How could I ever trust or feel safe in someone's arms if they could turn to forced sex when the mood took them? Now, I want to believe that there is someone out there who will have the patience and affection to put my needs on a par with their own. I have to believe that I can meet someone that I will be able to trust, physically and emotionally. Then, I just knew that my relationship with Sam had entered its final stage but that I didn't have the courage to end it. A bad relationship, *any* relationship would do – I could not be alone.

Over the next few weeks, I felt worse than ever. Something was wrong, not just with my mental state. I felt lousy, really tired and overloaded. I thought that if I could just have my period then I'd get back to normal. But my period was late and the pre-menstrual low dragged on.

The smell of cigarettes made me nauseous. Then it hit me. Oh dear God, what if I'm pregnant? No, I couldn't be. I pushed it away; there was no way I could cope, not now. I told Jess my worries and she took me to a clinic where I had a urine test. The nurse came in a few minutes later and said, 'I'm happy to tell you that you are pregnant.' I just sat there and bawled.

Later that day, I told Sam and he was elated. There could not have been a more ridiculous reaction – he was pleased in some way that he was going to be a father. 'Let's keep it,' he announced breezily, while thinking about his next joint. For a few hours, I was led by this reaction, just as I was always susceptible to being led by people with more self-belief than me. Sam told his mum and she said pretty much what I'd expected her to say, that we were on our own. Jess called round with Josh, a gay friend. I liked Josh, he was funny, but he also took the time to talk and was a sympathetic listener. I told them both what was going on and that I was not sure I could cope and that Sam kept saying, 'Please have the baby.' Then Dad called. I said, 'Dad, I'm pregnant.' Was I expecting him to be angry, to tell me it was not possible, I don't know. He congratulated me. It was insane. Sam hadn't a clue what he was asking for. He had no interest in working and providing for us. What would we do, end up in a council estate, with no prospects, just endless fights over drugs?

I could barely cope with my life; I couldn't inflict this on a baby. In the cold hours of one early morning, it hit me hard – I could not be a mother.

What could I tell the child about its family, about its

grandparents? In my heart, I knew that having a child would be a disaster, that I would wreck another life. If my mum had been alive, I would have gone ahead. She would have helped me and I would have gone back to college, regardless of whether Sam was in our lives or not, and I would have found a way. But not now. I did not have the hope or courage to carve some sort of life out of this despair.

Josh had a flat in Liverpool and worked in a video store. I said that I would travel to Liverpool and get a termination. First, I had to see a GP and I was then referred to another one. I told them both that I did not feel mentally fit enough to cope with motherhood. They gave me signed consent, but when I got to Liverpool, they told me my medical records were in Hull and that I would have to wait. By now, I was approaching my twelfth week of pregnancy and was desperate to end it. At first, Sam had no idea that I was seeking an abortion but with our return from Liverpool, I told him I was moving in with Josh and that he'd got me a job in the video store. He went crazy, but I left all the same.

On the morning of my appointment in the clinic, I sat with Josh and Jess, having breakfast. It was awful – on one level, I knew I was acting responsibly, how could I bring a child into this? On another, I'd been brought up my entire life to feel that abortion was a sin and I would not comfort myself with anything other than the hard fact that it was me who was deciding to end a life.

The staff were polite but detached. For them, it was a procedure but they can't have failed to notice how pathetic we all looked, sitting with downcast eyes, silent and scared. I discussed contraception. Incredibly, I had never used any but had never fallen pregnant. I was scared of the pill, in case I forgot to take it, and so asked for something permanent. I was told that a coil was unsuitable as there was a risk that I could become infertile. It is usually only prescribed to women who have completed their families, but I begged them and it was agreed that one would be fitted.

I was taken on a trolley and told by the anaesthetist to count to ten, but only got to four when I went under. When I woke up, I was taken back to the ward, still groggy, and Jess was there.

'Where's Josh?' I asked.

'He's been arrested,' she replied.

In the time I had been in the clinic, the police had arrived at Josh's flat and he'd been arrested for fraud. Apparently, he'd been filling out various student loan applications and pocketing the money with false IDs. I'd had absolutely no idea. But someone else knew: Sam, and after I'd left, he called the police.

I got back to Josh's flat but there was no sign of what had happened. I was bewildered, but at that point, I didn't know that Sam was the one who'd blown the whistle. The next day I went to work and people at the store were full of questions. I knew very little but was glad to be asked about Josh as it kept my mind away from what had happened to me. Josh's landlord turned up soon afterwards and I had to explain what had gone on and to beg him to accept that I knew nothing. He agreed that I could stay on at the flat. Jess was going to stay in Manchester with her sister. Dad called me and I told him that I had lost the baby. It was as much as I could cope with at that point. I was facing up to a new, if somewhat bleak future but I was relieved that I was doing so without the burden of pregnancy.

The shock of dealing with the fallout from Josh meant that I stalled in dealing with my decision to have a termination. On the day it happened, I woke up and the first thing I felt was surprise that physically, I felt no different. How was that possible? The baby was there and then it wasn't. At the back of my mind, I felt more than just a sense of relief. I remembered that a few days before the termination, I had put my hand on my stomach and said, 'Sorry, I am sorry but this can't happen.' I had the clearest sense that it was a boy, and I even started to imagine what he might look like and what I would call him. But a hard, animalistic, part of me knew that I could not raise a child.

Throughout the whole process, the most cruel part came when I went for a scan to check that I was less than 12 weeks pregnant. It was about ten days or so from the date set for the procedure and I did not want to watch the screen, but the nurse said 'Look.' I said I didn't want to but for some reason she was insistent. Perhaps that's what staff are trained to do, but when I looked at the shadowy, tadpole shape all I could feel was her disapproval. I said, 'Oh, that's lovely. Please can I have a printout?' and she seemed pleased. I was in turmoil. So many people seemed to urge me on to have this child, even this stranger who knew nothing about my life. She handed me the print out with a smile. I dressed, put it in my pocket and walked out.

The enormity of what I had done, choosing to end the

pregnancy, has never left me, but I would be a liar if I said that I grieved over my decision. I had grieved enough, enough to know the true depth of loss and this didn't come close. What remained was regret for a future I would never know, one where I could return home to Mum and raise a happy child. That future was lost to me, as was so much else.

I was working and that kept me distracted but it wasn't long before Jess started to appear at the weekends, offering a new diversion: pills. Jess would party for the whole weekend and although I suspected that she used more than dope, I'd always stayed clear of it. Now it was different. She was clearly high, but it looked like a happy and energised high. It was ecstasy and she said I should join her the next time she scored. I did, and this was the start of a new addiction.

You can hear every kind of warning about class A drugs, but when you see your friends taking them, having a good time, you think, I'll be fine. And of course, when you find that you are more than fine, that you are finally happy for those few hours, that life is good and you are free of anxiety, you want it time and time again. That pill is a guarantee that that night will be a great night. It was hard to work in a dead-end job, living from week to week, and saying 'no' on a Friday night when everyone else I knew was taking drugs and partying. It's just a part of the territory. I'd see government or health advice about drugs but it may as well have been in another language – there was a total disconnection to where I was in my life. I had to learn the hard way that a chemical rush doesn't come for free. The downside accumulates, and the days after the high start to demand a higher and higher price. I fell into bleak and terrifying lows but thought that all I needed was to climb back on, take the next few pills and keep going.

But I won't lie. Ecstasy is a rush – you feel bliss, you love everyone, everything is heightened and, most of all, you feel good about yourself. You feel invincible and that the party won't end this time. Work was a means to an end. I worked until Friday and then partied until the end of Sunday, as did pretty much everyone – it felt like a whole generation was doing the same. I'd become involved with another guy, a bloke from the video store I'll call Rich. He was a drinker and a coke user but I was playing out my old stupidity and walked into another bad relationship. The pattern was set from early on. He was absolutely fine when he wasn't wasted, good fun and a decent enough bloke. Rich was into me more than I was into him but I didn't care – I just couldn't stand to be alone and needed someone, anyone, to keep all my borderline terror at bay. Did I think I could cope when he lost it, when he'd smash his way into the flat and start yelling at me? Probably. It was what I was used to and maybe I thought it was all I could expect.

Sam had been to visit, begging me to come back to Hull and for us to get back together. Seeing Rich gave me a flimsy reason to hold out and say no, even though I was heading from the frying pan back into the fire. I didn't have the strength to reject them both and make a serious attempt to get my head sorted. Rich would get out of control, threaten me and push me around, all the time with me not fighting back, just waiting for it to be over. The next day, he'd have forgotten most of what had happened and he'd apologise over and over again, swearing it would never happen again. Then we'd get back to some sort of normality. I don't know how long this would have gone on, but it was Jess who was about to make a difference. She'd come over from Manchester and was pretty hyped up; she'd been told that there was a victim support fund available to people who'd been in situations like mine and that I could apply for it. She said that I should go along to the Citizen's Advice Bureau and find out more.

Jess was excited because she'd heard about quite sizable sums of money, perhaps thousands of pounds. She was sure that this was an answer for us both: we could move in together, afford a flat and splash out, start again with no men involved. I always found it impossible to resist her and anyway, perhaps it was an answer. I called Daiana and asked if she'd heard about the fund. She said that she had and that she'd received £5,000. Jess was thrilled, and the next day, I did go to the Citizen's Advice Bureau. They were very helpful and said that they would assist me with my application to the fund. I decided not to tell Rich; this was a potential lifeline and I thought that if the money arrived, I would leave for good.

In the meantime, the partying continued. We'd go to a club in Liverpool. Jess mostly preferred to visit and go out with me there rather than in Manchester. She was unstable on lots of levels, still prone to lashing out, but this made me feel all the more protective of her. It seemed even more as if we were in this together, no matter what men were on the fringes of our lives. She was the one who understood; she was the one I could rely on.

It was time to visit Dad. He had sent me money to cover the travel expenses and so I cleared a date. It was possible to stay in Rampton too. There was a secure house in the grounds, and families or visitors could arrange to stay overnight for £5. It had a communal lounge, similar to the inmates' lounge in that respect, but also a kitchen and a garden outside with a plastic climbing frame and a treehouse for children. I couldn't imagine bringing kids there. It's incredible how much your mind drifts away from facts sometimes. I'd think, imagine bringing a child here to see a murderer and then remember that's exactly what I was, a child on her way to see a killer. But I still struggled with the bare facts – almost two years after Mum's death, as time moved on, it seemed less and not more real.

I never reconciled myself to Dad being in Rampton and I would tell him not to talk to the other inmates. He once said that he was sharing a class with Beverley Allitt and I was horrified.

I said, 'Don't talk to her, Dad, please!'

'Actually, she's quite friendly,' he replied.

'But she's a murderer,' I said, getting more agitated, not wanting to think of Dad in the company of murderers.

'So am I, Natalia,' was his reply.

But I could not see it in the same context. These were people who sought out victims, children and even babies in Allitt's case, and chose to kill them. In my mind, rightly or wrongly, Dad was different. I honestly believed that he posed no harm to anyone else and that what had happened was a psychotic moment, a twisted need to possess Mum, and Mum alone. Even spelling that out, I realise it must sound odd or wrong. What was to stop him getting out and hearing the voice of God again and killing someone else? I couldn't answer that. I just knew that sitting with him over a cup of coffee, I could not believe that he was the same as these other serial killers.

But what I believed wouldn't have mattered to the staff at Rampton. They had to hear Dad repudiate his belief that God had instructed him; he would have to be stripped of his misguided faith. and so they were at loggerheads. Dad said he could hardly follow what they were talking about at his sessions with a staff psychiatrist but I wasn't so sure. He was one on the smartest people I'd ever met; there was little he had heard or read that he could not get the gist of and find counter-arguments. I think what they were asking him was to give up the one thing still keeping him sane, if that makes any sense. By not confronting what he had done, choosing to take Mum's life, he could just about keep himself intact. His belief that someone or something else made him do this terrible thing allowed him to still believe that he loved and cared for her. Expose him to the truth, and he'd crack and would never recover.

Plus, they never got to grips with Bruno's deep-rooted spiritual faith. He could talk to a Catholic chaplain and go to confession. To Dad, that would have been far more punishing than any group therapy session. In the confessional there are three, he maintained – you, the priest and God, and it is God's judgement that matters, no one else's.

His decision to resist the questioning from psychiatrists and to 'not understand' was his last and final defence. He had to keep their logic at bay otherwise he'd be like the others, like the boy who kept dropping to the floor or the man who lay on the sofa in Dad's communal lounge and terrified me with his moaning and rocking. 'Then don't look,' Dad would tell me. And I think that's what he was doing, choosing not to look into his own heart and the truth of that afternoon when he locked the doors of our family home and made his way from the kitchen.

This was the first time that I had seen Dad since the abortion. I had told him I'd lost the baby and his face was full of concern from the moment I came into the room. He had tears in his eyes and was full of sympathy. It was too much for me and I said, 'Dad, the baby wasn't lost, I had a termination. I'm sorry.' I broke down and he did too.

'Natalia, baby girl, what happened?' he asked.

I told him that I couldn't cope, not with Sam as he was. 'I'm sorry Dad,' I said. 'I got rid of it. I know it's wrong. I know now that I'm a murderer just like you.'

He was sobbing and nodded – he thought I *was* a murderer. In his eyes, abortion *was* murder. He looked up. 'You'll be OK now Natalia. I can't agree with what you did, but I love you. I won't ever be angry with you.' It felt like my heart was breaking. How did it come to this? The man who was offering me the greatest support had been my undoing.

But so much had changed. In my heart, I knew that he was no longer the man who terrorised my childhood. I had not forgotten Mum's words, that you can look beyond the act and look again at the person you love. Dad had not been there for me during my childhood but he had said sorry, and the more he made amends, sitting with me, telling me the truth, sharing his views but expecting nothing in return, the more I realised how much I needed a father. No one has a perfect childhood. Dad knew he had used violence and anger in a battle to control me, but it was different now. Now he was trying to be a better father, a better man, and I forgave him for the man he was in my childhood.

I returned to Liverpool. Rich was waiting, people wanted to go out and party. It's hard to explain how you can occupy a life and be so removed from it: you look from the outside and all you feel is disgust. I didn't go out, I wanted to stay in the flat, alone – another rare thing.

Within a few weeks, Rich had played out his last violent outburst in a spectacular coke-driven frenzy. He'd been out and came to the flat, and as soon as he was through the door, I knew I was in trouble. He was incoherent and I made the mistake of turning my back on him. He went for me. Picking me up off the floor entirely, he struggled over to the window and opened it. He said that he was going to throw me out. I was almost motionless, hearing his threats but watching his twisted face intently. When someone is on the verge of killing you, it's incredible how detailed their face becomes to you. I looked at his mouth, the spittle on his teeth, and the seconds slowed. Perhaps he would throw me. Part of me was struggling to care. That's fine, it will be over then. Would that be so bad? I don't know what stopped him. Certainly nothing I said or did. He was much bigger than me and I didn't struggle, so it was something that cut through his consciousness. We must all have that final mechanism to override, that tipping point when you move from anger to killer. He put me back on the floor and walked away. I went to bed.

I slept heavily. Not even adrenalin could keep me awake any more, I was closed off from everything I felt. The next morning, Rich knocked on the door. It was like a bad joke. Hello, I was the one who threatened to defenestrate you last night, remember me, your loving boyfriend? Rich may not have been the brightest man on the planet but even he picked up on my fear and confusion. What was he doing here? I told him about the night before. He looked shocked. I didn't know if it was genuine and I didn't care. He sat there crying his heart out, apologising and swearing that it would never happen again. It hit me then that I had spent half my life listening to men apologise to me. What was it in me that attracted such bastards? Did they just sense that here was a girl they could abuse and then pacify with 'sorry'? How many men had I seen sobbing before me, with fresh promises? It was too much. I lied to Rich and said, yes, I believed him, remembering that lying was familiar ground for me.

My life has always seemed to have a momentum rarely of my choosing. Events, personalities and conflict keep hitting me and I keep getting up and moving on. And the next push came with a letter from the Victim Support Fund. I would be receiving a cheque for £5,000. Our escape fund, Jess said. But escape to what? I had become adept at running and in my heart I knew that like a marathon runner, there was more to come. Jess said that we were going to live in Manchester; she quite liked it there now and had got to know a new group of people we could hang out with. Jess used up people at a breathtaking rate; she would ingratiate herself into new friendship groups, would work her way into positions of trust and then something would happen, usually to do with money or drugs, or both, and she'd have to move on. I don't know why she stuck with me. For whatever reason, for now I was to act as a constant in her life and she guarded me jealously. She looked out for me, of course, ever protective – she liked that role for herself – but she felt better around me the more fragile I was. It helped her to deal with her own brittleness. Two lost souls, remember?

The only sensible thing we did with the money was to put a down payment on a year's rent and the rest we blew. It was a new way to fund our distractions; we bought some clothes but spent it mostly on drugs. In the right – or wrong – circles, you'll be given drugs too, men hoping their generosity will pay off. I was given coke quite a few times but luckily it never really got to me the way I saw it get to others. Mostly, it was pills I hungered for, that quick shift to numbness. Then I'd get up and dance; it was so easy.

When Monday came around, I'd go back to my life of temping, working in various offices in the city. I needed to keep earning money and work was a good distraction although I was never interested in staying in any job for long with the idea that I could 'progress'. Work was just a means to an end, a way of getting cash together and funding what happened at the weekend. Living with Jess was OK. She liked having me on hand to go out with on demand, or to stay in and watch TV and talk with – we'd order pizza and do our best to switch off. Everything I'd learnt from Dad was proving too much. I had pushed it aside; it felt like the only way I could keep getting up in the morning and commuting to a job where I'd answer phones and make photocopies. I'd walked back from the cliff's edge. I knew in my heart that it wasn't over, and that it could only be avoided for so long but I had to keep putting one foot in front of the other.

Months would go by before I could see Dad as Rampton was so hard to get to, but we'd write and I'd call him. I still have some of the cards I sent to him. Looking at those cards now, I'm sure other people would struggle to understand them. One card talks about the world being short of heroes, and goes on to say, 'I think about how much I look up to you. I've got my very own hero, and always have.' They are gushing and signed off with me saying, 'This card says it all. I love you so much and miss you so much, your baby girl, Natalia.'

One card also thanks this dad for being someone 'I can talk to and share my soul with. Thank you, Dad, for your praise and patience, for teaching what you could and letting me learn a lot on my own. You encourage me to believe in the best.'

And I could talk to him and share my soul. What I'd learnt on my own had almost destroyed me – at 21, I had a life burned by abuse and mistrust, and I couldn't hold down a healthy relationship with a man, good or bad. I was a wreck, but I truly yearned for life to be different. Yet with Dad, I had become the daughter he'd always wanted: loving, loyal, affectionate and guided by his advice. And he was a dad that I always knew how to find, who would listen without anger and would tell me, his 'baby girl', how loved she was.

One thing I wrote has a deeper meaning that I did not see at the time because I was still too consumed by need and grief. I wrote: 'Without you, my world would crash. I love you more than words can say. I appreciate you in my life every day. I miss you so much.' And it probably would have crashed, had we not managed to find a way to invent this new relationship between father and daughter. It wasn't a love more than words can say, it was a need: we were both at the edge, we sustained each other. I would sit and hold the hand of the man who had killed the one good thing in my life and I would hold it like a lifeline.

But what was the alternative? I had enough of my mother's heart in me to fear hatred. I sensed that it could consume and destroy me entirely; my destructive use of drugs and men would go into freefall and I doubted I would see 30. My admiration for Dad might have been built on a lie but I was not strong enough to carry on without him in my life. I had to believe that my life could be different, that sharing my soul did not have to mean despair but the best life had to offer.

Time was moving on. I realised that I was drifting into my mid-20s and yet I was failing to make more of my life, but there was one change and a good one too. Shaun had tracked me down and asked if he could come and visit. I was thrilled as I had liked him for such a long time and knew that he was a decent bloke. He came and stayed at the flat one weekend and within minutes it was as if we'd never stopped talking. He knew about everything that had happened with Sam but always had the knack of making me feel good about myself. He was a quiet man, who would smoke, but that just made him more laidback, and he was just so easy to spend time with.

We went out partying with Jess but I think neither of us was interested in being out – we both wanted to get back to the flat and spend time alone. I fell for Shaun very quickly. He made my life feel uncomplicated and before too long, I'd find myself wishing the week away so we could be together again. He was still living in Hull and he worked in construction. He earned decent money and treated me so well. We'd go out to eat and he'd buy me things. It didn't matter what they were – he just made me feel special. For the first time I started to believe that I could trust someone. He would listen as I talked about Mum – he had the rare gift in men of being able to listen rather than waiting for a pause and jumping in with some sort of 'you should do this' suggestion. The emotional mess of life doesn't interest most men; they prefer to work out a 'solution' and avoid the rest.

There was only one problem with this new and happy love affair: Jess hated it. She hated that I was so wrapped up in Shaun and was verbally aggressive to him every weekend. Shaun was the kind of guy who would never think about lashing out, even verbally, and so I thought he was cool with it all. But I was wrong. It was putting pressure on him, I suppose, particularly as I didn't try to stop Jess. I had such a blind spot where she was concerned, and always would.

Things came to a head after only about six months. We'd

come home early one Saturday night and had moved the TV, which was in the living room and belonged to Jess, into our bedroom. We'd watched it and fallen asleep. The next morning, Jess got up late and came into the living room to see her TV was missing. Without saying anything, she marched into our bedroom and unplugged it. She strode back into the living room, where Shaun was sitting, and threw it at him. She threw it at head height but Shaun was quick enough to dive out of the way; she went ballistic, ranting and raving.

I was shocked and tried to ask her to calm down. Shaun picked up his things and walked out. Perhaps I should have followed him, gone with him, instead of staying and remonstrating with Jess. I think it must have upset Shaun terribly. When he called, he said it was over between us and that he just couldn't deal with it any more.

I was desperate. 'Shaun, don't worry, I'll move back to Hull,' I offered.

'You can't, Natalia,' he said. 'Sam is still here.'

Sam had no idea that Shaun had been seeing me. We both knew that he would make our lives impossible.

Part of me thought that Shaun would change his mind. I lay awake praying that he would. But he didn't, and I was heartbroken. I had loved Shaun. I had not done enough to protect what we had and it was a lesson hard learned. For me, this was a new and raw pain, waking up and knowing that I would not see him that weekend. Jess was happy; she told me that she had not been able to handle that he had taken me away from her. I felt trapped. Shaun did not want me enough to start somewhere new. He told me that he had dreamt of taking me away from the mess I was in with Sam, but now he left me with Jess, someone hell bent on her own destruction. I couldn't be angry with him. He was a genuinely lovely man but I had not carved out enough space for us to survive.

But Shaun never lost touch with me. Even to this day, he still calls me to see how I am. That has given me more faith than he will probably ever know. He's happily married with young children and I think his wife is very lucky. It's strange how different lives can run alongside each other for a while, and even reach out and touch, yet you know they won't stay that way for long. Shaun, despite the drugs and the partying, always seemed the one who'd be able to leave it all behind, to veer off back into a normal existence, where things like family and future are taken for granted. He's a good guy who saw what pain I was in, and although he couldn't help me change that, he has had the heart enough not to forget. He even helped me fix my broken-down car one weekend, years after we stopped seeing each other, driving more than 100 miles because I was afraid I'd lose my job if it wasn't working by Monday. It gave me hope that there could be another Shaun out there for me.

Shaun's decision to end our relationship was tough at the time and the realisation that Jess and I had used up all the money the Victim Support Fund had sent me only heightened my anxiety. I was starting to find Jess's possessiveness harder and harder work, and being short of cash didn't improve the mood in the flat at all. But, typically, rather than trying to walk away on my own, I was waiting for the next person I could attach myself to. It was by chance that I bumped into another school friend, a girl called Amy, who was at university in Wolverhampton. She was living in Stoke-on-Trent and suggested that I visit her for a weekend. I was ready to jump at any chance to move on, any kind of distraction would do. Amy was grounded; she enjoyed a pretty wild social life but at the back of it all was her determination to finish college and get a good job. I've always admired people who have a strong sense of purpose, something that eluded me. And I don't think it's about what kind of home life you come from. To be unhappy at home is never ideal but it provides plenty of people I've met with determination too. Daiana has drive. She worked her way steadily up through her career in management and is clearly someone who has used her past to push herself onto bigger and better things.

From time to time, I would talk myself into thinking about going back to college, about trying to plan a better future as in my heart of hearts I knew that I was alone, and that it was up to me to make changes in my life, to support myself. But at the same time, I allowed myself to find the next guy, waste his money and think no further than the next party. Perhaps I hoped being around Amy might make a difference but whatever the rationale I gave myself when I moved in with her, it wasn't to be.

I was at a party and the DJ – I'll call him John – took an interest in me.

We soon hooked up. He always seemed to have a ready supply of pills and coke and would know what event to crash. At first I was taken in with all his talk of DJing at VIP events and acting as a driver for celebrities but it wasn't long before I figured out that he was a seasoned liar. I'd call him up when he was supposed to be at a nightclub and it was clear he was at home. He always had a tale to spin and I once asked him why he made stuff up: he answered, 'If I didn't, I'd be dead boring otherwise.'

I met his mum and she was just lovely. It made me realise that even with the most caring of backgrounds, some people are destined to go off the rails. At one point, he got busted by the police, who alleged they found he'd stuffed his underpants full of Es (ecstasy). I can remember cringing when I read the headline. But he got off and was soon back DJing. He could act in a really daft way, but sometimes he'd deliberately set out to scare me too. One night, he banged on our flat door and he was nursing a package.

He looked pretty frantic and said, 'Natalia, you've got to help me! You've got to hide this for me. Don't ask any questions.'

'What is it?' I shrieked as he pushed past me towards the bedroom.

'I've told you, no questions!' he yelled. 'I've been involved in something, I don't like it but it's serious and you have to hide this for me. Say you'll do it.'

I nodded dumbly as he stuffed the package at the bottom of the wardrobe and he rushed out. I was terrified. What if it was a murder weapon? I wanted nothing to do with it. I called Amy in and was in tears, what was I to do? She looked in the wardrobe and carefully unwrapped the bundle: it was a gun, a toy one. She almost collapsed with laughter but I couldn't believe it. 'It's not even real,

Natalia,' she laughed, but then again, very little of what John did was real.

Perhaps life with John should have been funny but I was in no fit state to navigate what was reality and what wasn't. The drugs I had taken were taking their toll – the highs were shorter and the down periods becoming longer and longer. John loved to drive. We'd take pills and set out on some road adventure or another, usually driving in and around North Wales. We wouldn't get out; we'd just drive and drive, listen to music and I'd chatter endlessly. Then John would go very quiet and I'd start to worry. He'd look angry, murderously so, and would cut in with something like, 'Natalia, you've really pissed me off now.' I'd ask why, getting more and more worried, my mind scrabbling around trying to think what I might have said or done to upset him. I'd be in tears and he'd say, 'What is it? I'll tell you what it is. It's you, just you – you piss me off!' I'd break down. The crash from a drug high can be terrifying – all your usual rational barriers have imploded and you are locked into paranoia and self-loathing. Then John would laugh and say ,'Ha ha, I was only joking!'

It was too much. I could put up with the petty drug dealing and the stupid lies but my mental state was just too fragile to cope with any more. I sat with Amy and told her that I wanted to die. It was the blackest of depressions and I could not stop crying. I said, 'Look at my life, look at all the bad things that have happened to me and there is so much more to come. I'm young, but I can't cope with any more. I can't do it.' And I meant it. The idea of finding the fight to get back up was beyond me. If I'd had a way to push a button and end it all then, I would have – I had nothing left.

Finally I was picking up the tab for my drugs misuse. It's like being a gambler – you have early and easy wins, and then the need to stay or get back in the game takes over. There's no enjoyment any more – all you have is the hunger and the chase, the illusion that you can get back to where you were and enjoy the rush. But the stakes get higher and higher, and you lose control. After a few days, I picked up the phone and called Daiana. 'Please come and get me, Daiana,' I said. 'I'm a druggie and I need your help. Please come and get me, you have to save me.' Saving me was beyond what I could ask of my sister, but she came the same day. She asked few questions; there was no tearful scene of reconciliation. I blubbered all the way back to Scunthorpe but Daiana kept her composure, again sensing that the burden of care had fallen to her again.

I was so grateful to her; I sat and told her that I had been using drugs but she was matter of fact, saying, 'Look, Natalia, I know I probably drink more wine than I should – we all have some crutch or other. Just stop now and you'll be OK.' She didn't want to discuss it further; she felt that forcing me to look ahead and move on was the best remedy. One joy of being back in Scunthorpe was living with Daniel again. He was in his early teens now and although he'd changed so much, to me he was still my baby brother. We'd lie on his bed, and laugh and hug each other, and I felt for the first time in a long while that perhaps I could turn a corner.

I looked again at college and enrolled on a business and

admin course. I wanted to be positive about my next move, but the picture at home was not as peaceful as I'd hoped. Daniel had moments when he was his old self, but I could see that he spent more and more time feeling troubled and unhappy. I tried to put it down to the usual teenage angst but there was more going on beneath the surface than my sister and I realised. He wasn't enjoying school and I think he was struggling to come to terms with the idea that he might be gay. I would look at him and then push aside all that he'd been through in his short life; it was too cruel. When he'd say something like, 'I don't think I can remember what Mum's voice sounded like,' it just broke my heart.

An obvious source of antagonism for him was the fact that my sister now had a boyfriend. Daniel hated the idea and the fact that he often monopolised Daiana's spare time. Not that she had much of it. She was dedicated to Daniel, and his desire to ice-skate; he shouldered all the responsibility for caring for him, and so I was glad that she had found someone to date. Daniel would make a huge fuss if he was at the house so Daiana spent more time at her boyfriend's flat, while I stayed with Daniel. With me around now, Daniel took the chance to give his school my number and told them it was the number to use, should they need to speak to someone. He asked me to pretend that I was Daiana, if the school called, so I should have guessed that something was going on.

I was working in a supermarket and had started my course. The only problem was getting from my shift on the check-out to the college – the walk was over an hour, but

I felt it would be worth it. I was pretty clean-living at this point but still went out with Amy. She got hold of me to say that there was a huge dance festival planned at the NEC in Birmingham and I agreed to come along. It was great, a fantastic escape, and I ended up chatting to a bloke called Steven from Aylesbury. He got my number, and even though we lived miles apart, he seemed determined to see me again. I wasn't that interested, but he called once as I set out on my way to college. When I told him what I was doing, he stayed on the phone for the whole hour. He said that way he was making sure I was OK. I liked that, and it became a regular thing – I'd walk from work and Steven would chat to me until I safely reached the campus.

He was keen for me to come to Aylesbury but I wasn't sure. It seemed a backward step, just following the next bloke who came along, another man I wasn't even in love with. So I said no, and just thought it would fizzle out. My course was going well and I was sure it would lead to something but then I got a call from Daniel's school. They asked to speak to his guardian and I said it was me. The voice on the phone said, 'I'm sorry to say that we found Daniel in the toilets at lunch time and he had cuts on his arm. They didn't require stitching, but they were bleeding, I'm afraid.' I felt ill to think of Daniel in pain, but kept my voice calm, keeping up the act, so I thought.

I was frantic with worry until Daniel stepped through the door. More than anything, he looked embarrassed and my tears didn't help. He had cut his arms. I held him, and asked him over and over, why? 'I don't know,' was all he'd say. I told him that we could not keep this from Daiana; he'd have to tell her and we'd have to get help for him. When Daiana came home, he did tell her. She asked the same question as me, why? When Daniel used the same reply, she said, 'Well, don't do it then.' I was gobsmacked. This wasn't facing up to the crisis Daniel must be in, but it had an echo of when I first arrived at her house. I would spend the mornings in tears, wrecked from weaning myself off pills and dope, and Daiana would ask me why I was crying. When I said, 'I don't know,' unable to begin to articulate how bleak I felt, she'd say, 'Well, don't do it then.'

I have no doubt that Daiana loves Daniel unequivocally, more than a sister, as she has also been his mother. I know she loves me too, though this is something we never talk about, but the way we face life is so different. I hit problems head-on, or lie and lick my wounds until I can get back up and face them again. Daiana is ruthlessly practical, seeing my emotional outbursts as an indulgence she can ill-afford. I wish with all my heart that living with her could have brought us closer, but it had the opposite effect: my presence seemed to bring greater chaos.

The final straw was a dreadful fight I got into with Daniel. Daiana had gone for a night out with her boyfriend and I was looking after him. From the moment she left, he became more and more agitated. He said that he wanted to call her and tell her to come home, that she should be there and not out. At first I tried to reason with him, and then distract him by saying that we could watch TV together or talk, but Daniel wasn't interested. He was getting increasingly worked up and I did the wrong thing by raising my voice and telling him that he wasn't allowed to call her, that he was being stupid and that she deserved to have time for herself.

I honestly thought he'd see reason. Daiana was only going to be out for a few hours and it was silly for Daniel to expect her to nurse him around the clock. But it was too much for Daniel. He wanted to grab the phone, yelling that he had to know right now what time she'd be back, but I stood in the way. It turned physical, with neither of us backing down, and I lost my temper. There was no way I was going to let him phone Daiana and he knew it. We screamed insults at each other, both of us nearly hysterical. I pulled the phone socket out of the wall but then Daniel snapped. Totally. He ran to the kitchen and picked up a knife, screaming, 'I'm going to fucking kill you, just like Dad killed Mum!'

In a blind rage I threw myself towards him. I hurled him to the ground and banged his head against the floor. At that very moment, Daiana opened the door. She is an unflappable woman but this was too much; I honestly think she could not believe her eyes. Daniel and I looked half-crazed. I wasn't scared of Daniel as much as I was angry, but seeing Daiana snapped us both back to our senses. She wanted to know what on earth was going on and when I tried to explain, she said, 'Natalia, you should have just let him call me.' She was her usual matter-of-fact self and I felt that I had managed to mess up again hugely in her eyes.

I went to bed and before too long Daniel came to see me and we hugged, cried and apologised. Even now, he and I will somtimes row but we are never mad at each other for long. Sooner rather than later, one of us will pick up the phone and we'll talk through what happened, say sorry and that we love each other, and we'll move on. But that's now. Back then, Daniel was only 14 and he was a lot more fragile. Even though we'd made up, I didn't fully appreciate how much Daiana thought I was hampering rather than improving things at home. Although she had been calm when she went to bed, it must have caused her genuine worry about the months ahead because when I woke up, there was a note pinned to my door. It said: 'Natalia, I really don't think this is going to work out and I think you need to find somewhere else to live.'

She'd gone to work but did not come back that evening. Daniel spoke to her and it was clear that she would stay at her boyfriend's house until I had cleared out. On one level, I couldn't blame her. On another, although I appreciated that my sister would always be a safety net for the family, it was clear to me that she wasn't going to be my crutch: I had to find my own way.

She had done the same with Emmanuele. She did not need extra dependents and eventually he had found a girlfriend, with whom he had moved in. She was right. I was an adult, not like Daniel, and I should stand on my own two feet. But I would be lying if I said that I did not feel some despair. It had been five years since Mum's death and yet at 24 I seemed to be drifting, with little purpose in my life. It should have been a moment to stop and take stock, and perhaps retreat from everyone until I could find a way to start afresh. But as I walked away from what remained of my family, I panicked. Where could I go now? I supposed I would have to call Steven.

CHAPTER ELEVEN

FINDING A WAY OUT

I'm lucky enough to have friends now, good friends I can trust. Whenever I'm with them, I know that it's OK to have made mistakes. It sounds so simple but it's something that I've had to learn the hard way: to find myself at a crossroads and, for once, to take the right path. Not to repeat the same mistakes, or follow old patterns, to even have the courage to reinvent my life.

Reinvention might sound a little rich, like I'm Madonna planning a new world tour. That's not what I mean – I suppose what I mean is that it took me a long time to realise that everyone make mistakes, even terrible ones, often when they're young, but that it's OK, it's allowed – it's part of life. Time after time, I would choose the wrong men, the wrong friends, and it wasn't because I expected things to work out this time, it was because I had no idea how else to behave.

My childhood wasn't easy, I knew that, but what I didn't know was that I was carrying a destructive legacy and allowing it to pave my future. I've no doubt now that if I had carried on as I was, I would have lost my mind and quite possibly my life. I was on a downward spiral once again when I hooked up with Steven; it wasn't a smart move but after leaving Daiana and Daniel, it was all I could think of. We found a shared house to live in and I went through the motions for a few months. I'd see Jess, she'd come down from Manchester, often only because I'd send her money, but it didn't bother me – it was part of my obligation to her.

Jess's philosophy regarding men was clear-cut, 'Find them, use them, fuck and chuck them'. I thought it was funny but I didn't think it was how I behaved; I didn't think I was using men, but in a way, I was. I didn't let them anywhere near me emotionally, even if it was a sexual relationship. I remained distant – they served a purpose, earning money and keeping me company, but even when I heard, 'I love you', it meant little other than feeling slightly more in control.

Steven swore he loved me, but I withdrew further and further until at last, he gave up and moved out. The only good in my life at this point was that I had met Jo. She worked alongside me in Greggs, the bakery, and I liked her straightaway. But this was a very different friendship to the ones I had had before because if Jo didn't like the way I behaved, she'd tell me. She had a huge amount of integrity but I found it tough to handle at times. It was Jo who first suggested that the way I treated men wasn't healthy, that I would push and push to see what I could get away with, only to recoil from anyone who stood up to me. To be honest, I could not see what she meant at first. It was only when I caught myself coyly saying, 'Oh, go on, make me a cup of coffee', in a voice that sounded like a little girl's that I remembered my Dad's manipulative demands, and how he treated Mum.

I was at a point where I could imagine that in a relationship only one person could ever be in the driving seat. If anyone let me walk all over them, then I could not respect them. But at the same time, I would not walk away from men who used violence against me. In part, it was all I knew. I seemed locked into a see-saw of extreme relationships, playing the bully or playing the victim. Steven and I had split up in early 2002, and I found a place of my own in another shared house. Then I did the best thing I could possible have done – I shut myself away. I went to work, saw Jo, but stopped partying and stopped seeing men. Night after night I would stay in, and I had to learn how to be on my own, something that terrified me. In the first few weeks, I hated it. Constantly being with others, people I didn't truly trust was its own drug. It kept the adrenalin flowing, not knowing what would happen next. If the drugs were bad or the company volatile, it stopped me thinking abut myself beyond the next few hours. Being alone, sober and with no distractions was truly horrible in those early weeks; it was a withdrawal.

But I knew I had to do it, that I had to find a way to be comfortable with myself and just learn how to stop. I started growing up, I started to realise that with no solid understanding of who I was, I was so easily led. It was a slow process but it was the right thing to do. They were hard months but they proved vital: it was my first real attempt to spend time away from all my frantic efforts to keep running from the past. At the same time, I was seeing less of Dad. I wrote to him and we'd speak on the phone but the distance was a problem as I still didn't drive.

I'd love to say that this was how I turned the corner and that it's been plain sailing from then on in but life is never simply plotted. I still had a few episodes to endure before I could truly stop making basic mistakes in relationships and learn how to take better care of myself. There was still one final fall I was yet to make, where I thought it would be best to end my life. It was some way off and yet I suppose the warning signs were clear to see. I had changed jobs yet again and moved, and one of my new housemates was a guy called Jay. He was lovely but I made it clear that I would not get involved with him. Nevertheless, he introduced me to his mum and I found that I just adored her. She was so lovely, listened easily, never judged and was very warm and caring. In truth, I fell for her rather than Jay. I would call her, take her out for lunch and drop by for tea all the time.

She was in a tough relationship herself and over time, she told me that she was planning to leave her husband. I told her not to: I said that I could not handle the idea that something awful would happen to her, that he might do as Dad had done. I think it shocked her, the idea that I thought it inevitable that women are vulnerable, and that by leaving, husbands were likely to become murderers. For now, she stayed; she let me call her Mum and I think she hoped for the best for me and Jay. But we weren't compatible. We ended up in a house together, as friends, until the day I got a call from Jess. She was in serious trouble, she owed people lots of money and needed somewhere to hide, and so I didn't hesitate to ask her to stay. That meant we were a bed short so I agreed to share with Jay. I must have been mad if I imagined that he wouldn't try it on, and sure enough he did, but I just went along with it; it was a mistake but it worked for a while. Pretty soon, I could see that he was plagued by insecurity over our relationship. He demanded that I didn't talk to other men but would happily flirt with girls. I remember how embarrassed I was when I was chatting to one of his friends and he angrily grabbed my leg and said, 'That's *my* girlfriend.'

It just seemed so childish, but there were no lengths he wouldn't go to. Jess planned a holiday for us both in Ibiza and as soon as Jay found out, he booked a holiday for us on the same week. He made me choose between them, but it was his choice of destination that was the greatest shock – he'd booked a holiday in Brindisi, my dad's home town. He knew all about Dad, and that this was where he was from, but it was the last thing I expected. The two of us travelled to Brindisi, and it was the strangest of holidays. I told my dad's older brother, Franco, and he was there to meet us. The week was a whirl of visits to relatives who were often very upset about Bruno, all conducted in Italian; it was very intense. They had immense curiosity about me, the daughter who 'stuck by her father', but I could not even begin to talk to them about all I now knew and felt about Dad.

Two things stayed with me: An aunt's shock at seeing Jay iron his own shirt. Even in the twenty-first century, she saw a woman's lot as little more than housekeeper and actually stopped him, finishing it herself. It was like stepping back in time. The other thing was how little there was to do in the town: it was a harbour and little more, no pubs and clubs or a social scene. In the evening, going for an ice-cream was about all my relatives could suggest. The only thing that stood out from what was often a drab existence was the churches: they were magnificent. Walk inside and they were awash with gold and colour, stained glass and ornate altarpieces; they overload your senses. No wonder Dad was awed by what he saw, and carried some of that with him all his life. Dad thought it was wonderful that we were there. I sent him a postcard and told him that I wished he was there too, and a big part of me meant it. I wanted to understand, and Dad still held the key in so many ways.

But week away had done nothing to help Jay and I resolve our differences. The harder he wanted to hold onto me, the more I wanted to escape. I did, in the most foolish way – into an affair with a guy I'd met, Toby. It wasn't that I was in love – I was just amazed at how laidback he was. I went to visit him and he didn't start pawing at me the way all the other men I knew seemed to do. He could sit and talk, and that was that. Starting an affair was easier than telling Jay it was over. I didn't want to confront him as I didn't want to hurt him but on top of that, I was terrified of losing his mum.

But with Jess's return, much of the effort I had made to spend time alone began to unravel. I stupidly told her about the affair and before too long, Jay knew. It was catastrophic; he was incredibly upset and broke down in tears. I ended both relationships: I was paralysed over what I'd done, repeating all my old mistakes and now despairing of ever crawling my way back to some sort of peace in my life. I moved out. Jay pleaded that we get back together but the real shock was Jess's attitude – she was more hostile than Jay. I remember calling the house they still shared and hearing Jay crying in the background. I begged him to stop, but Jess grew angrier and started screaming abuse at me, ending with, 'You really are such a nasty girl, Natalia!' It was as if something broke inside me, like a piece of machinery that was overused and then grinds to a halt. Jess and I had always protected each other, for good or bad, no matter what we did or how we behaved, but now she had turned on me.

I was exhausted. Parts of my mind and body were simply shutting down and I was numb. I had lost another Mum, I had hurt everyone around me, the one girl who promised to stick by me hated me and called me a nasty girl, I couldn't take any more. So I went to bed. It was a weekend, everyone in the house, people I barely knew, was away. I sent a text to Jo and Daniel telling them that I loved them very much. Then I switched off the phone and took a huge handful of paracetamol.

I was 25. I didn't want to live any more; it was too hard, I could not cope. I faced a life of caring for Dad, knowing I would not see Mum again and I was simply defeated. I closed my eyes; all I wanted to do was to sleep and not wake up. I thought about the time when I had come home from school: it was bitterly cold and Mum had called me into the front room. Every bar of the electric fire glowed a warm orange and I lay down, tired but happy, watching Dad stroking Mum's hair. The TV was on, no one spoke, and those few seconds watching them remains the one time I felt truly at peace at home. I drifted into that moment, happy that I would soon see Mum again.

I woke up vomiting. My stomach was gripped with violent pains, and I didn't know how long I'd been unconscious. The phone was ringing but I didn't want to get up – I doubted that I could. It rang and rang, stopping me going back to sleep. In the end, I crawled into the hall just to make it stop. At the end of the line was Jo, asking me what was going on; she felt panicked as my mobile was off, something I'd never do. I told her what I'd done and she came straightaway, putting me in her car and driving me to the nearest hospital.

Nursing staff can have little sympathy for young women who've overdosed, and are perhaps frustrated with a medical emergency that is self-inflicted. They were professional but curt, and seeing what a state I was in, still throwing up, they said there was no point in pumping my stomach as it was too late. After checking what I had taken, I was put on a drip and told that I had to wait to see a doctor. I slept a little and when I woke up, my stomach still raw, asked when I could go home. I was told that I couldn't until I'd seen the doctor and the psychiatrist on duty. It cut through the haze I was in and I was truly scared. There was no doubt in my mind that if I stayed, a psychiatrist would try and have me committed to an institution. Everything I had seen in Dad's hospital flooded through me and I was terrified; there was no way I was going to stay. I pleaded to leave but it fell on deaf ears, so I took the drip out of my arm. It bled and soaked into the long-sleeved T-shirt I brought in with me but I didn't care. I was on the first floor and was determined to jump out of the window if I had to. I snuck out of the hospital – no matter what happened to me, I vowed myself never to end up somewhere like Dad had.

Back at the flat, Jo stayed with me for a while and I promised I wouldn't do something as stupid as that again. I would not answer the phone as I was too afraid that it was the hospital. Jo told Jay what had happened and he called round, very upset, and asking that we get back together. I cried with him and begged him, 'Jay, please help me end this relationship – I can't take it any more.' I think then he realised how far I had fallen and just how much we failed to help each other. He agreed that from that point on, we would only be friends.

I didn't tell Dad that I had attempted to end my life. I didn't have the strength to put myself on the rack again about how and why I had done it; I started to realise my limitations and that I could not keep exposing myself emotionally. All I could manage was to block out what had happened. I don't know if that was the right thing to do, I don't know if anyone can ever successfully bury a truth about themselves but for now, the best I could do was to forgive myself for that one time, for failing to get up and fight. I had to learn to take better care of myself and to just give myself a chance to heal. I knew that I was a long way from being well and whole, but for the first time I started to trust in time a little more. Terrible things had happened

217

but terrible things did not have to be all I was. Perhaps I could have a normal life, a life where I was more than the daughter of a killer, the girl who had had her mother's life taken by the one man she should have trusted, the girl who had seen the worst in men, who knew what it meant to live without a home and see friends turn on her. Why did I have to be that girl? Perhaps I could be someone new.

With Jo's help, I began to get some balance back in my life. At first, I was too nervous to contact Jay to ask if I could see his mum but within a few months, he began to text me and he would chat to me if we passed each other in the street. One day, he said, 'Why don't you call Mum?' I went to see her, this second mum, and realised that she could be a friend, but not my mother. It made me realise how deep the scar was, losing Mum, but rather than let it distort the relationship I could have with Jay's mum, it would make me face up to it with a little less hurt. She wasn't my mum, but she was a force for good, an older woman's voice, there to always extend a welcome. It is a dangerous thing, to try and fill a need with a substitute, and it can't last. I had to learn that Mum was gone and that there would be no other mum, but that it would be OK in time. I would learn to honour her in my own way, not by trying to fill the void.

Another positive step was learning to drive. That meant it was much easier to see Dad without the hassle of public transport or relying on others. I had moved jobs too, this time to a bed company, and for the first time, I had taken the time to get to know someone before agreeing to go out on a date. His name was John and he had a great sense of humour. The time in work was fun as he always found a way to make us all laugh. He wasn't the best-looking guy in the world but I realised that when I saw him, when I walked into work in the mornings, it made me feel good about the day.

We started seeing each other and I thought how lucky I was to meet someone so kind. The year that followed was a good one. John and I did all the things that couples do: we'd go out and eat, shop and cook together, and watch TV. I loved how bland and uneventful our time together could be; it felt great. He knew about Dad. I knew it shocked him but he seemed genuinely concerned and to be someone who wanted to help me put it all in the past. I visited Dad when I could, sometimes driving up there with John. I would tell him that I wasn't able to come, making up one excuse or another, and then I would turn up as a big surprise. He'd be amazed and it would reduce him to tears. We'd sit and talk about Mum over coffee, and if anyone passed us, we would have looked like any ordinary dad and daughter. Around this time, Bruno was told that he was moving to a medium security hospital called Greentrees Lodge, near Hull. It meant that he had a little more freedom – he could walk around the grounds and could even walk, with me, to a café on an industrial estate that bordered the hospital. I had to come to terms with the fact that Dad was unlikely to face any sort of life except in an institution but this was a big improvement on Rampton. They are some of my happiest memories, just being able to spend time in an environment that was close to normal.

It has never left me, the realisation that Mum would not be able to enjoy such simple pleasures, and knowing that has affected each of her children in different ways. We each had to deal with what was left of our lives. Daiana chose to treat Dad as a dead man – that was her way of denying him any more control over her life – and when she heard that he was being moved to Greentrees she decided to leave the area. It was too much for her, the idea that she could bump into him on one of his escorted walks. Daniel was yet to reach a decision on whether to see Dad; he was still so young. I found out that Emmanuele had visited him, along with his wife, but I didn't know how he was coping.

In an ideal world, Dad and I would not have been forced into the relationship we had through his brutality; we'd simply be a loving father and daughter. But that wasn't to be. We had found a way to be together and now he never abused my trust in the way he had in the past, and for my part, like Dad, if I promised something, I would do it. I never pretended to forgive him for all the things he had done to us but I promised to listen and not to let him die alone. The past was closed and I had to learn to live with the consequences but I had a choice to make – the choice of how to live. I chose to try and be a decent human being and act responsibly towards him, but at no point did I pretend that he had not killed Mum.

I thought about the neighbour who had cursed me for staying in contact with Dad. I remembered that she had said that Mum would have turned in her grave. All I could hope was that somehow Mum might see that I was doing the best I could, that I was behaving in a way that she had tried to teach me – living with compassion and love and hope.

Life was never going to be perfect but I at least could end

each day thinking harder about what I did and what I felt, and try and take a step back and not be so reckless. This was wholly new to me. I didn't have to be the angry young girl hurling from one bad moment to the next; I'd stepped out of my old life – I suppose it's how many people try and cope with things that happen in life. I'm sure it's what Mum felt for so many years, that if she just tried harder and honoured and obeyed Bruno, her old life would heal and the future improve. The difference between Elva and me was that I had seen the bad things for what they were and stepped away from them. She never could. And it was through listening to Dad that another piece of the puzzle came to me: he put Elva on a pedestal, he truly did. He didn't love her; he loved the idea of the fallen girl that he had transformed into an honourable wife and mother. He thought he knew and loved her, but what he cherished was his own invention – he didn't really know Mum at all, none of us did. She was imprisoned by her past and by her marriage, and I had had a glimpse of who she was and who she could have been. She was lovely, funny, wise and caring but her life had been stunted by men with the worst desires.

That would not happen to me. Never again would I put myself in a situation where I would be hurt or neglected or abused. But the crucial lesson I had learned was not to be an abuser of people either. I would wake up with nightmares that I was pregnant – the idea of being a mother terrified me. What if I was like Dad? What if rage spilled out of me and I acted as he had? I would be in a cold sweat, wondering if I was a monster. It was as if my mind was testing me, unsure of the new territory I was moving into;

it was testing the ground beneath my feet, how much I had changed and moved away from my childhood.

Life could have carried on like this for many years, I suppose but, of course, life rarely stays unchanged for long. In 2005, a new crisis came with a phone call from Dad and the news that he was unwell. Within weeks, I was once again thrown into turmoil. Bruno would not be getting better this time: he had been diagnosed with cancer of the bladder and now he needed me more than ever.

CHAPTER TWELVE

LOSING DAD

There's a lot to be said for a regular life, a life where you can pretty much predict what you will be doing this time next week and even this time next year. I think it's the bedrock of what keeps most of us sane. Yes, you can worry that everything becomes too dull and predictable but that can easily be changed. I've been searching my whole life for a home life that I can take for granted as something safe and dependable; it might seem that searching for an ordinary life is strange but I can say that truly, if you have never known it, it is hard to find.

I think that's what I was trying to create with John and, to some extent, I mimicked it pretty well. We were together for two years and from the outside, it must have seemed like the life many young couples lead. Both of us were working and caught up in all the detail of a nine-to-five lives. I thought less about my past and more and more about the small stuff, such as how to find the money if my car didn't get through its MOT, where we could afford to go on a two-week holiday in the summer, or whether to find a new job.

Now, I realise that I never took enough time to step back and look at how one event after another had marked my attempts to build relationships. I had lurched from one crisis to the next. Just getting by was as much as I could hope for but even during life with John, a regular life, I never risked an examination of how damaged I was. I just got caught up in the day-to-day and I welcomed it – I didn't want to think about my past any more.

Hearing that Dad was unwell was like slamming into a wall. My carefully-made new life was shattered by the interruption of my old one. Once again, I was the daughter of a killer, with the responsibility of fulfilling my promise to be there for him. Having a routine life with John meant that my past didn't fill my head so much; it was good, but it hadn't faded completely. Whenever I met someone new, just a friend of a friend or a new work colleague, I would tell them, often during our first meeting, that my dad had killed my mum. People never knew how to react – some would move off the subject as soon as possible and were clearly uncomfortable; others would want to know more, with eyes wide open. I had my few prepared answers but Jo wanted to know why I insisted on telling everyone. It didn't take me too long to figure out that, in a way, it was a defence mechanism. I couldn't stand for someone to find out and talk about it behind my back. My way, I'd meet it head-on and feel I was more in control.

But I wasn't fully in control and I was soon to learn that my past could still have the power to upset my hopes for my life. From time to time, John would complain that I kept him at arms' length, that he could never get really close to me. I'd shrug it off and say that I didn't know what he meant. But I did. Part of me was terrified of being heart-broken again, the way I'd felt over Shaun, and part of me just didn't know how. Being intimate was hard for me. I'd never been shown how and very often would lurch from being very distant and defensive, desperate not to be suffocated by someone needing me, to clinging to men like a limpet, saying, 'Tell me you love me, give me a hug, don't go, stay here with me.' There was no easy balance I could ever find. I was doing the best I could with John, hoping he'd take comfort from all the things we did together, nights in watching television and shopping trips; we had a routine and I was happy with our lot and I prayed that would be enough.

Yet Dad's illness shattered everything, like a mirror smashed into a million pieces, I held the fragments but what I saw was fractured and made no sense any more. I was a daughter, sister, lover, once again but I was being pulled apart in all directions. Daiana did not want to see Dad. My brother Emmanuele and his wife were visiting but this was adding new tensions; his wife seemed to be competing for his attention and it took on a new and vicious twist as the months went by. Daniel was pulled too, not wanting to upset Daiana, who meant the world to him, but also feeling the need to say goodbye. He would talk with me and I sensed that he wanted to settle things with Dad once and for all, but more than anyone I knew that confronting the facts of your life was a double-edged sword. I told him to think it over and that I would be there for him if he wanted me to pick him up and take him to visit Dad.

The first time I saw Dad was dreadful – I was terrified of what I'd see. Would he look ill and frail, and expect me to hold him and soothe him, telling him he'd be OK? I had no idea what I'd see and even less of a notion of how I'd cope. I'd only spoken to him on the phone in the week since he'd told me he was ill and he'd tried to be as reassuring as he could, saying that he felt fine and that he was sure he'd be OK. But the fact that he was passing blood when he urinated made me worry that the cancer was more advanced than he realised. Dad was frail, but there was no question that he would be considered for release. He did not want me to visit him in hospital; I had offered to go with him for his chemotherapy but he refused, saying all it involved was lying down with a drip in his arm, so he didn't see the point of dragging me all the way to the ward in Hull. I'm not sure of his real reasons for not wanting me there – perhaps he wanted to spare me, perhaps he was too afraid himself and did not want to have to put up a front for me. But he was adamant and there was never any point in trying to change his mind.

Walking in that first afternoon, what I mostly felt was relief. He looked tired and thinner than I remembered but he seemed in good spirits. He was sitting in an armchair in the lounge of his shared flat, and he held my hand quite happily and chatted as he would have donw if nothing had been wrong. I asked him again about how he felt and he just said, 'I promise you, I am going to be fine.' I started to believe him. Being there with him, I just wanted to put on a brave face too and join in with the game of 'nothing has changed'. I talked about work and John, made jokes and kept everything upbeat. All the while, the illness was like an elephant in the corner. I hoped that by ignoring it, I could defy what was happening. It was clearly what Dad wanted and I was happy to go along with it too. I didn't want to dwell on what it all meant, that he would die there in a mental institution, a condemned killer, leaving a broken family of orphans. It was too much to deal with, here, holding the hand of the man who had brought so much destruction and yet had meant so much to me over the past few years.

That tension was proving too much for me at home. I withdrew further from John during the one time I probably could have opened up and asked for his support. The turmoil I was in brought all my worn and scared defences to the fore again, and I would snap at him over nothing, finding any excuse to lash out and lose my temper. He tried his very best to be patient and to understand what I was going through but he stood little chance. I couldn't understand it myself. My dad was the man I had wished dead for most of my life, and now that he was seriously ill, all I could feel was a fear that something would happen to him. I knew there was a storm coming, that he was the last link to Mum, and that should he die, I would feel dangerously alone and the full weight of Mum's loss would hit me again. I did not think I had the strength to mourn afresh and so I was hanging on to Dad's reassurances while pushing John further away. I just didn't believe in John enough; I didn't trust him enough to let him help me.

After a month of chemotherapy, Dad said he was sure the cancer was beaten. He had lost a lot more of his hair and quite a lot of weight but said that he was positive that he had turned a corner. I was relieved. I think we all were; it was as if we had cheated the inevitable collapse that would follow Dad's death and we could go back to the sort of normality we'd established over the years. I would visit every couple of months and we'd carry on reminiscing about Mum. John could see that I was happier, but by now he was tiptoeing around me like he was walking on thin ice. I hated that I had created an atmosphere at home where he had to gauge how I was feeling when he walked into a room, sensing that I could flare up at any moment. The idea that this was how Mum had had to live tore into me but I knew no way to back down; I was as much a prisoner of my emotions as John was. I hoped that Dad's remission would mean that I could start getting my life back onto an even keel and perhaps repair the hurt that John felt.

On a visit to Bruno, about six months after his first diagnosis, I could see that he was failing to gain weight and looked uncomfortable when he was sitting for too long. I asked what was going on but all he'd say was that his back was giving him trouble. My stomach lurched. I think at this point, we both knew that what we feared had come to pass, that the cancer had returned. Dad was re-examined and it had spread aggressively, this time to his lungs, liver and kidneys. There would be no renewed course of treatment – Dad would have to prepare himself for the worst.

He was calm. I sat with him and asked, 'Do you think this is punishment for what you did to Mum?'

'Yes,' he replied simply, and he seemed resigned to the fact that he would die. I asked if he was scared and he said no.

Then I asked, 'Dad, if you go, will you find a way to come back to me and show me that you are OK? If I stand in front of a mirror, will you come back and show me that you can still be with me?'

'I will try,' he said, 'but I don't think that God will allow it. I don't think anyone can return after death. But I want to ask something of you: I want you to do something with your life, Natalia – do something that you think you can't, not all these dead end jobs. Try for me, I want you to be happy.' I don't remember my reply.

The kindest thing the hospital did was to arrange for Bruno to visit Italy to say goodbye to his family before he died. I was angry that they would not release him entirely but this was a gesture that I appreciated, I thought it was the humane thing to do. I can imagine that years ago, if I was told that tax-payers were helping murderers to go on a 'holiday', I would have been outraged. But I've since learned that there is far more than one side to every story. Allowing Dad to go to Italy, to show a man like him compassion and dignity is what sets us apart as a society; it shows that we are better than those we have to lock up.

He was given an escort from Greentrees and was grateful to have the chance to say goodbye to his brothers and sisters. My uncle Franco was amazed. A few years earlier, he had tried to find out if there was a way Dad could be moved back to Brindisi to serve out his time. It was a possibility as Bruno still held an Italian passport and Franco was pleased with the idea that his brother could be close by and cared for by his family. I was worried at the time that it would mean I'd hardly see Dad at all but I did not stand in the way. Perhaps there was a part of me that welcomed uncle Franco sharing some of the burden.

But a few months later, when uncle Franco called me, I could tell he was in shock. He had been to visit his local secure hospital and was horrified at what he found. The conditions were very poor, the buildings unclean, with ten men to a room – he said that he even saw rats in the hallways. He decided that Bruno was better off where he was and vowed to visit each year instead. He kept his word and I think he appreciated that conditions at Rampton befitted the name of 'hospital'. If you judge a country by how it keeps its prisoners and its mentally ill, I think, on the whole, that Britain can hold its head up.

Dad's health was deteriorating but he was determined to say his goodbyes. The hard fact that Mum had not had the same luxury was not lost on me but I had to keep thinking about how she would have wanted these months to be. Mum had no bitterness in her heart, even when she'd found the courage to leave him. One of the things that inspired me was the lesson that she tried to teach me, to live by the best impulse in your heart, not the worst. Dad had been enslaved by the worst. I wanted to live in a way that my mother would have been proud of.

Dad called me from Brindisi and he seemed happy, as if he was letting something go. There was no doubt it was an emotional time; there were tears from everyone. My Italian relatives can be emotional but I wondered what else they were mourning – their beloved brother had grown up to become a killer: did they feel any guilt too?

No doubt there were some who blamed my mother, believing Dad had 'snapped' after years of living with a 'disobedient' wife. It's easy to hide behind the idea that women bring punishment on themselves, and more common than you think. Yet I'm sure Dad's visit would have given some of his relatives cause to reflect on their own lives, and it wouldn't have been easy.

When Dad arrived back, he was in a wheelchair. It was as if he had held back all his remaining strength for the trip and now he had nothing left. I was shocked when I heard his voice – it was cracked and broken, barely a whisper. I called Daniel as I sensed the end was near and that there might not be much time for him to make his peace with the past. I wasn't sure what to do – he was torn. He had not seen his dad since the day of Mum's murder. Part of him wanted to look him in the eye and realise that he was a weak and old man, not someone who deserved to be feared anymore. I half-expected Daniel to tell Dad that his illness was justified and to show him how miserable he had made his beloved youngest son. But Daniel was not angry, just very subdued when I spoke to him on the phone, and he asked me to call him back in half an hour.

John still wanted to comfort me but I was fixated on Dad and Daniel; I just excluded him all the more. I didn't know if I was doing the right thing. What if it made Daniel feel so much worse about the past? What if Dad still had the power to say something destructive and leave Daniel in turmoil? There was no way Daiana would be happy to see Daniel with him; in her mind, he was already dead and she wished to have no part in mourning what was left of him. The phone rang and it was Daniel. He said, 'Natalia, I want you to pick me up and take me to the hospital. I want to say goodbye' All I could do was say OK, and so the next day I drove up to Nottingham and waited for Daniel in my car. I didn't want to risk a confrontation with Daiana. She may not have said anything, but I was taut with worry about Daniel and felt it best to avoid any conflict. Daniel was very quiet on the journey. I knew he was overcome by what he expected to see and feel, and I just told him to expect Dad to look very poorly and no longer like the man he last saw when he was 9.

We entered the hospital and I was anxious as I knew that we would be watched for the whole of our visit. Dad was not allowed to be left unattended, even though he was terminally ill, and a member of staff was present. Some were discreet and would read a newspaper or retreat to the back of the room; others weren't so accommodating and I would sometimes feel antagonised by the presence of a complete stranger taking a ringside seat to watch our family's misery. When Dad saw Daniel enter his room, he broke down. He said 'sorry' over and over, and 'thank you'. As much as he had fortified himself over the years with ideas that what he done to Mum was out of his control, at a moment such as this his defences crumbled. As Daniel stood before him, he was crushed and all he could do was replay the sorrow he'd stored over the years. Daniel was so brave. He was in tears too and told Dad that everything was OK; it was all he could do. He could not pretend that he forgave Dad or that his actions had not torn his life apart, but facing a dying and broken man, saying that he was OK was as merciful as it was possible to be.

Dad talked about dying and told us that he was not scared and that we should not be afraid either. I asked him where he wanted to be buried and he said next to Mum. I told him that it wasn't going to be possible as Daiana had bought the plot and there was no space allocated for him. He asked instead if I would take a handful of his ashes and scatter them near Mum, and that the rest of his ashes be returned to Italy. I said that I would carry out his wishes, and in the back of my mind, the betrayal I had shown Daiana by bringing Dad's flowers to Mum's funeral came to me and I felt a familiar unease. Yet, in the end, I also remembered that Elva had not removed her wedding ring after leaving Bruno, and neither had she changed her name back to Winfarrah. I decided that a handful of ashes was probably right; he had been the father of her children, the one thing she treasured above all else, and so it would be a symbolic gesture to her as well. Mum may not have had the best from this man and had suffered the ultimate betrayal, but I could not pretend that he did not matter to her while she lived.

Dad then took off his wedding ring and offered it to Daniel. Daniel said he did not want it, so Dad passed it to me. I already had Mum's engagement ring and realised that I would be keeping a part of them together now. I'm not proud of the way that I came to get hold of Mum's ring, though. It was a ring I always loved when I was little and I used to nag her to let me see it and try it on. She also told me that when she was gone, she'd leave it to me. After Mum's death, I asked Daiana about the ring but she said she didn't know where it was. Years later, after I begged her to collect me from Stoke and she was good enough to take me home with her, I went searching for something – I forget what – and I came across all of Mum's jewellery and so I took the engagement ring. I was angry that it had not been given to me but also too embarrassed to confront Daiana. I have it to this day and my sister has never asked me about it.

The staff at the hospital told me that Emmanuele and his wife were visiting too. But I didn't want to see them – I was too raw. Emmanuele's wife and I had clashed over Dad, which was just ridiculous. She sent me a text saying that she was a better daughter to him than I had ever been as she had given him the one thing he'd wanted: grandchildren. I was completely floored by this. In the midst of all that was going on, it was too much. I had no fight left in me to deal with any kind of confrontation. I was exhausted, but worried that I would snap. At least I had the good sense to know by now that I could not rely on myself to stay rational so that seemed the smartest thing to do, all in all.

My life seemed to be imploding. Too much was happening, too quickly and I was struggling to keep afloat. John had asked to visit Bruno too and eventually I had agreed. At this point, we'd been together for two years and so it was only natural that he wanted to be there for me – even though I was keeping him at arms'-length, perhaps he thought that by being at my side, he could convince me to let him be there as support. But Dad had other ideas. We walked into the hospital room and he struggled to set himself upright, his face a knot of rage. 'Get him out, get him out of here!' he yelled. 'That man is going to hurt you! Listen to me, Natalia, he will break your heart – you must listen, get him out!'

I was horrified. Dad was so agitated, as if he had had a vision, but he was aggressive too and I think that if he could have got off the bed, he would have thrown John out of the room. John had the good sense to back out but he was as shaken as I was. We did not talk about it; in fact, most of the journey back home took place in silence. I could not even begin to sort out all the events and emotions that kept hitting me. Dad had frightened me, and I found it hard to look at John.

The last few weeks were the worst. I had to get back to work and couldn't afford to stay in Hull. Part of me sensed that Dad did not have long but even when my head told me to prepare for the coming weeks, in my heart, I was struggling to imagine coping with being alone again. I was in the library on a Saturday, only a few days after last seeing Dad, when my mobile rang and it was the hospital. They said that Dad had taken a turn for the worst and asked that I drive up to be with him. To his credit, John came with me. The journey was so hard – part of me was concentrating on the practicalities of driving on a motorway, while the rest of my brain kept collapsing into worry about what I would see and how I would cope. I was moving at 80mph, but at the same time stuck in one paralysing moment, waiting for the end.

When I saw Dad, it was worse than I had imagined. He

was painfully thin, as if his body was sinking into itself; his skin was grey and he wheezed painfully. He looked nothing like Dad; he looked like a corpse and I was terrified. I picked up the cottonwool soaked in water that was on his bedside table – a nurse had told me that this was the best way to give him a few drops of water. As I looked around, I saw photographs on the wall that I had never seen before: pictures of Mum taking communion in Brindisi, pictures of Dad when he was young. Dad's psychiatrist came in and I asked him about them. He said they were among Bruno's things and he had wanted to put them up. I asked if we could keep them after Dad had gone and he said that he thought it was unlikely. That puzzled me, so I asked why and he told me that it was because Dad had recently changed his will and that everything was going to Italy. But to me that seemed unlikely – surely he would have told me?

I looked down at Dad; his lips were cracked and his skin seemed like paper over yellow bones. I held his hand and talked to him. I asked him to squeeze my hand if he could hear me but there was no response. I don't know how long I sat there listening to him as he struggled to breathe but a tear then ran from the corner of his eye. It was too much for me.

I said, 'Dad, I can't watch you die. I'm sorry, I can't be here and watch you die. I can't wait and listen for your last breath, I'm sorry. Please go to Mum and give her my love. I miss her, I'll miss you too.'

I was trying to breathe through my sobbing and had to get out of the room. A nurse told me that Emmanuele was in a waiting room but I couldn't see him at that moment. I sat in my car for some time and then started the engine. What I had said to Dad had been true enough – I could not watch him die. I called the hospital each day, more than once. On Tuesday, I called and the ward sister said, 'He's just gone.' Three words was all it took to change my life once more. Mum and Dad were both dead now and I would have to find a way to live with that. I was glad that Dad was no longer suffering but knew what lay ahead. First, I would have to hold myself together through the funeral, and then, the hardest of all, get through the days and weeks and years that lay ahead.

John had been talking about us getting a house together. I was sleepwalking through most of what he had planned for us but I was grateful that he could think about and imagine our future together. The funeral followed a week later. I visited Dad in the Chapel of Rest and was shocked. He looked nothing like Mum had; it was like something out of a horror movie – his lips were black and he was completely sunken. I backed away from the coffin and could not look again. It was an awful day, grey and gloomy, and I was in turmoil about how I was supposed to feel. I knew Dad had loved me and I knew that I had loved him, but the destruction he had brought to us all by taking our mother from us poisoned so much. I tried to keep sane by remembering the grace my Mum had always shown. So many people had attended her funeral, as even in the brief time that Dad would allow her to spend with others, her goodness shone through. She was always sympathetic and kind; she had a loving heart. I wanted to honour her by remembering what she had tried to teach me and what I had rejected for so long.

It couldn't last. I knew that no matter what face I could present at the funeral, I had a storm of emotion to battle through. And my composure slipped more quickly than even I could have guessed at. After the cremation, I asked Dad's psychiatrist, who was also acting as an executor of Dad's will, for some of his ashes. He said no. I was bewildered, and so I began my explanation of why I wanted them. He said it was out of the question as Dad had left everything to his brother Franco and that everything, including his ashes, was due to travel to Italy. I began my story of why I wanted them again but when I realised that my pleading was getting me nowhere, I lost it. The psychiatrist was impassive, no doubt he was a veteran when it came to clients and their relatives going into meltdown. I was railing against him for nothing.

My anger spent, I felt powerless; I would not be able to keep my word to Dad. I don't know how I got through the next few weeks. I kept functioning but was tearful and confused. After another attempt by John to get us back on track, he asked to speak to me and sat me down to say that he no longer thought that getting a house together was a good idea. Even as I was listening to him, I was struggling to appreciate what it all meant. He said, 'I don't want this any more, Natalia. You won't let me in, you never have, and I've never been able to work you out.' I could see that he was exhausted too and feeling huge guilt over telling me but I understood that it was true that he could not take it any more. I knew that throughout our relationship, I wanted him there as a source of comfort and a way to avoid being alone, but that I had never really wanted him, not as a lover should. Everything he said made sense, but I was in no fit state to deal with sense.

Thinking about John, Mum and Dad should have been the trigger points that led me to tears, but they weren't. I was on a downward spiral but even my grief now seemed to be set against me. I could not cry when I thought about the people I had loved and lost but I would be tearful over stupid things – just from being tired or unable to hold one thought together after another. I could no longer block it out and carry on as I had so many times before. I had hit a wall and I was going down; I couldn't get a grip and feared for my sanity.

I went to my GP and asked for help. I said that I wanted this over.

She asked me a series of questions: 'Are you crying constantly?'

'Yes,' I replied

'Do you feel sad and depressed?'

'Yes,' I replied.

'Are you struggling to cope day to day?'

Again, my reply was simply 'yes', and what the hell else did she expect to hear I wondered? She prescribed me anti-depressants, not something I had really sought, but I was at the end of the line. I was given Citalopram, the anti-depressant used to treat depression associated with mood disorders.

It had been six months since Dad's funeral and as the days stretched before me, I saw the task of getting on with life as harder, not easier. Mum's death had taught me that. The second year and the third year don't mean time is healing you – you just find a new and hardened form of loss and hate the fact that this is your reality, for the rest of your life. I would never see Mum again and would not be able to cry and laugh with Dad as we relived our best times with her.

I had to drive to work and part of the journey took me onto the motorway. I had been on the anti-depressants for one month and I felt wretched. In my car, I started to have vivid fantasies about death. I would imagine a rope tied around my neck and attached to a lamp-post and then how easy it would be to put my foot on the accelerator and snap my neck in two. That would be one way for all this to stop and the idea felt logical. Depressed as I had been, I was sure that these hallucinations were down to the drug I had been prescribed. In the flat, I flushed them away and went to bed. Within 12 hours, I started to withdraw and had stomach cramps and flu-like symptoms; it was as I imagined cold turkey might be. I was genuinely scared and at one point when I got up, I felt light-headed again, and I stumbled, falling down a few stairs. I managed to get back to bed and lay in a cold sweat for a few more hours.

Withdrawal left me with a feeling of nausea and a spectacular bruise from crashing out on the stairs but it did make me vow to myself never to touch anti-depressants again. Once again, despite my desire to give up, the stubborn part of my brain was making me face facts: I was in this on my own and I would be the one who had to find a way out of it. Enough was enough. I don't know where that stubborn need to hang onto life and keep moving forward came from. At first I thought it was from Dad. He was immovable once he'd made up his mind and would work like a dog to provide for his family. He didn't know anything other than standing on his own two feet and fighting his corner.

But then I realised it was just as likely to be Mum. Elva, who had dealt with trauma from an early age, who had made the wrong choices about men and ended up in a marriage which far from offering her salvation, had eroded her confidence and belief in life. But she had done all she could to keep her children together and had the most forgiving heart of anyone I ever met. She would want me back on my feet; she knew me like no one else, not even Dad who had learnt everything about how I had been hurt and how I had messed up a thousand times. She knew that I had to learn everything the hard way, putting my hand in the flames and listening to no one. And Mum had told me that she believed in me even when I didn't believe in myself.

Mum had loved me, with an open heart. Dad had shown me how love can destroy goodness but he had shown me the truth, and he had told me to stop wasting my life. And then Daniel phoned, with some truly amazing news. It was just what I needed – it was all I needed to try once again.

EPILOGUE

A LIFE ANEW

When you sit down with a blank piece of paper, it's fairly easy to chart what happened, and to create a line of events that shapes a sort of story of your life. But, of course, to live a life is very different. It's messy, for no two members of the same family will remember events in the same way – it's impossible, it's too personal, and memory corrupts as much as it recalls.

Until recently, I had always assumed that Mum told Daiana everything. I was envious that she was close to her in a way that I wasn't – as Daiana was older and not disruptive, and she spent hours with Mum in the kitchen. Daiana was surprised by this and pointed out that much of the time Mum spent with Dad, she was depressed, too depressed to share chit-chat and share confidences with her eldest daughter. This made Dad's act of murder all the harder to bear for Daiana because now she would never get to know her mother fully; it was Dad's ultimate punishment, she felt. That's why he was dead to her from that moment. She goes by her married name, although divorced, so there is no link to her father and she says that she does not hate him, as hate is a passion – rather, she feels indifferent to him. It is her way of cancelling him out, and something I have never been able to achieve.

My memories of the house where we first lived in Scunthorpe were mostly happy ones. I asked my sister what changed to make the next house so much harder to exist in. Again, Daiana had a totally different recollection of the house; the atmosphere was no different to that which I grew to hate. Perhaps I was too young to understand what was going on around me and certainly too young to start standing up to Dad. And having conflicting memories doesn't just apply to our state of mind during a time or place, we even have different memories about specific events, like the day Mum moved in to of the flat in Cleethorpes. Daiana tells me that she arranged for the removal van when I could have sworn it was Aunty Jean. We are both the daughters of Bruno and Elva Aggiano but Daiana's story would be very different from mine.

Daiana is ten years older than me and after Mum's death, when my life went into a tailspin, there is no denying that the impact on her life was very hard too. Her marriage ended and she effectively became a lone parent with Daniel to care for. Emmanuele and I both used Daiana too, knowing that she'd be there to run the house and be responsible, just as Dad had always demanded of her. Despite claiming that he was suffering from 'diminished responsibility' at the time of Mum's death, the fact that he picked up the phone to tell Daiana what he wanted her to do still causes me a chill. He was entirely clear-minded at that moment.

That's why Daiana never accepted the claim that he was mentally ill. She saw nothing to suggest otherwise. My sister also had to learn to be tough with my eldest brother and me. Quite rightly, she would not let us live off her indefinitely and made us both face up to our responsibilities as adults. But she could not do that with Daniel. In some ways, this must have been her greatest burden: where I was free to sweep in and out of his life, she was the one who had elected not to have children and yet she was charged with his care and schooling. It can't have been easy and yet it also proved to be the turning point for all of us.

Daiana didn't just love to skate, she moved into coaching and proved an inspirational teacher. She worked incredibly hard to get all her qualifications, while holding down a full-time job and caring for Daniel. Skating proved to be a strong bond between the two of them, and she was there to help Daniel bring his talent into view. When Daniel called me, it was to say that he had been skating with a new temporary partner and that, irony of ironies, she was Italian. Her parents were so impressed by what they saw in Daniel that they suggested that he should think about following them back out to Milan to take a place on an intensive course. What's more, one of the coaches from the Italian squad had seen him skate and because of Daniel's dual heritage, he said that if he worked hard enough, he could even earn a place in the squad.

My sister speaks fluent Italian and Daniel does not, but there was no doubt in her mind that this was a fantastic opportunity. He travelled to Milan with Daiana and despite his anxieties about the language and cultural differences, was told that his goal of gaining a place in the Olympic team was well within his grasp. It was the most fantastic achievement, especially when I think of all we grew up with and all the setbacks he has known. I'm so incredibly proud of him and my sister. For me, it was a turning point, just knowing that Daniel was making something of his life, through his and Daiana's hard work. And he was still so young, only 18. When I remembered what my life was like at 18, what Daniel was doing made me feel both humble and very grateful – perhaps Mum was the guardian angel I always imagined she could be, after all. Daniel is funny, loving, very hard-working and lights up every room. Yes, he can be as combustible as me, but after loud or angry words, he never hesitates to pick up the phone, to apologise and talk everything through. He is a mix of my Mum's grace with a little bit of Italian exuberance too. I think Mum would be incredibly proud of him and every time he goes out to skate, he sends a kiss towards the skies for her.

My sister found that she was now in a position to give up her office job and coach full-time. I know it's a job that she loves and I'm sure she'll nurture even more young stars and bring lots of happiness to adults who want to learn to skate, too. Ten years after Mum's death, I don't think any of us could have predicted a life for ourselves after that day. I'm hugely proud of my brothers and sisters: Emmanuele has a family and I know that's where he is happiest. I'm not going to pretend we are close but we see each other from time to time and there is no ill feeling between us.

My only regret is that Daiana and I aren't closer. Emotionally, we are chalk and cheese and I just have to respect that. I'm gushing, often over-emotional and I think it drives Daiana to distraction. She is far more measured and controlled. I'll text her saying 'I love you, I hope you are well. I'm missing you', and she'll reply 'I'm well. Hope you are OK too.' We just misfire in each other's company. I don't think she trusts the way that I live my life – she's seen me make too many mistakes and cause too many scenes to let her guard down yet, and I can't say I blame her. Growing up, I was the troublemaker, she was the peacemaker; I could lose my temper and lash out, but she was the one who had to keep her emotions in check for the greater good of everyone else. If you met me, you would never guess any of this. I'm always smiling and ready to laugh. I'm easy-going, even if I speak at a hundred miles an hour – I think that's the Italian in me! And I never get into any conflict or arguments, if anything, I'm the first to back down or walk away. But when I'm with my sister, I feel like a teenager again. We end up in our old roles, and I just know we're going to rub each other up the wrong way. All I can do is give it time and accept that we face the world in different ways.

Hearing Daniel's good news gave me cause for hope and Dad's plea that I do something with my life has not left me. Something about this rang true: I had never believed in myself enough to push myself and take a risk where work was concerned. When Dianna took me in, I had tried to go back to college, but my fight with Daniel meant that I walked out on it. But that was five years ago and if college had meant enough to me then I would have simply re-enrolled in Aylesbury and got on with it. It was time to sit down and really try and figure out what I could do with the rest of my life.

I sat down with a blank piece of paper and with pen in hand tried to think about what interested me. It might sound crazy but I wrote down 'something to do with airports'. I can't claim to have spent much time in airports but whenever I have, they've intrigued me – just the idea of so much human activity, sometimes millions of people flowing through one place at one time, and heading to destinations I've often never heard of. I switched on my computer and typed in something about 'jobs in airports', not really expecting anything in particular to come up. Within a few seconds, I was led to a site where there was an advert for people to work in airport security. There was an assessment form to fill out to see if you were suitable for interview. Straightaway I wanted to know more and so I sat down to complete the form. It was a good job I was sitting down as completing it took ages – it felt like I was being asked everything except what knickers I was wearing! But it left me hoping that I would hear back from them, until I saw to my horror that the interviews were for 8.30am the next day. It wasn't going to happen. I had to pick Daniel up from Nottingham and take him for his flight to Milan, leaving from Luton at 4am.

When the email arrived to say that I had been accepted for an interview, I was so disappointed, but I had to put it behind me as Daniel came first. After picking him up, I told him about the interview and he was adamant that I had to go. It was ridiculous as I had been driving for hours and didn't think I could get to the interview in time but Daniel made me promise to try. I honestly thought I wouldn't bother – I was so tired and I was sure they'd take one look at me and show me the door. At the last minute, I turned off for Heathrow and thought, what have I got to lose?

I arrived at the hotel at 6am, which left me with a two-hour wait for the day to begin. When I walked into the foyer and saw that the coffee shop was open I gave a huge grin of relief; I thought that coffee was my only hope of staying awake until we were called in! I was quietly hopeful at first but as it got nearer to 8am, I started to worry about just how many people were entering the room. There were a hundred applicants and it was quickly made clear that most would be eliminated as the day progressed. My heart sank. I'd never be able to come through it I was sure.

Half way through the day, there were only 50 of us left. We'd been through written and verbal tests, and had been given fact sheets to revise things like X-ray machines and procedures. I'd never done well in exams in my life; I would read work at school and as soon as I put the book down, would forget everything. If ever I needed help it was now. Perhaps it was Mum, because when it came to sitting the tests, I was able to plough through.

Each time the numbers were whittled down, names were read out and the candidates were thanked and shown out. Those left went through to the next stage. It was 5pm and my name was read out along with three others. I was so disappointed, to have got so far and no further. But then the examiner said that those four names were the candidates who had been successful and he thanked everyone else for their time. I could hardly believe it: I'd made the last four out of a hundred and I honestly would never have dreamed that was possible.

That was October 2006, and I was placed on a provisional contract, sitting further exams and assessments until I passed and took a permanent contract in February 2007. The training has continued ever since and it's a job that I truly love. I wake up each day and look forward to joining my colleagues: they are a great bunch of people and I feel more at home here than I have anywhere. The role relies on shift work and that can be hard, switching from nights to days and so on. I have to be really disciplined about when I sleep but I wouldn't change where I work for the world. Something about the role just appealed to me: I knew the work would be varied and interesting, and I felt as if I was making a real contribution to keeping the airport, the airline crews and the passengers safe. Working has also meant that my life has started to feel mine for the first time. I'm earning decent money and supporting myself – if I have shoes on my feet, they are there because of me and no one else. This time, when I make promises to Daniel, I keep them, such as buying tickets for Daiana and me to fly out and see him. It has meant so very much to me.

People at work know about my past. Again, I wanted to be the one who told them, not have them find out. Everyone has been really kind and supportive. I left Aylesbury because the commute to Heathrow took too long and moved into a shared house nearer work. The house is great and I feel that I have the basis of a safe and happy home life for the first time since I was tiny. So much has changed over the last few years and I have learned that change never stops. It would be too easy to be caught up in my past and let it define me and how I behave forever but I know that's not what Mum would have wanted. I don't know if she could ever have found it in her heart to forgive what Dad did; that is something I will never know.

It was also in 2006 that I was introduced to something that helped me frame all I felt about Mum. A friend told me that there was a memorial site online where people build pages about their loved ones and where you can add pictures, thoughts and memories. It is helpful because you can visit when you feel low and there are others online who know how hard it can be to live with grief. There is always someone there to send messages of support or a few hard-won words of wisdom – people you never meet, often from the other side of the world, but all linked by what it means to lose someone you love – something none of us can avoid as we move through life but something we cannot prepare for.

When I saw the site, I knew it was something I wanted to do for Mum. It was originally an American site but now users from all over the world post memorials there. I had to learn how to construct a page, completely new territory for me, but in a way I found it therapeutic. I was learning something new and it cleared a space in my mind to just think about Mum and all she meant to me. Now I can log on and say to her, 'I'm feeling down today Mum, you'll know why', and I'm sure she does. You can see Elva's memorial at www.elva-aggiano.memory-of.com.

As for her four children, we were given so much by Mum and she made the ultimate sacrifice. Alive, she endured her unhappiness so that we might stay together. The idea of losing her children was greater than any tyranny she had to go through with Dad. She tried to break away but his fear and rage destroyed her in the end, and that is the moment I cannot forgive.

But I remembered her words to me, her plea that I don't forget the lessons of love: that it is possible to love someone for who they are and not what they do. It was painful, but despite my bravado, I had to come to terms with the fact that I had always loved and needed to love my father. The violence and control he used against me as a child turned my need to be loved into something dark and it cast a shadow over my early life. Nevertheless, in the end, despite all that had happened, he offered me his love and his apology. He taught me that love can endure anything but that the human heart is all too often edged with fear – fear of rejection, of loss, of betrayal. Dad's weakness was to let those fears contaminate his love. He tried to control and manipulate those around him, those closest to him, those he held dearest and it nearly destroyed us all.

I think it would have done so, had it not been for my mother. She was the one who showed me that to love truly means to love without fear; that love needs to be given freely and unconditionally. It's a lot to ask but it's no more than the human heart can give.

It has been a hard road and I have known moments of

desperation, of pure anger and rage, and times when I wished life would end. But that is because I hated what I had learned, feared what I had become and was scared of the scale of what lay ahead of me. It's no good trying to put the past behind you without facing up to it first. You may think that by closing it off, you are free of it, but I have learnt that, left unchallenged, your behaviour will still be coloured by the same fears and anxieties. I see now that Mum's traumatic rape led her to such unhappiness. No one listened to her or helped her, and it led her to her own destructive behaviour. When Dad came along, she thought she might be free of the shame she felt but instead, he wrapped up her 'sin' into his own fears and used it to trap her into an unhealthy marriage, isolating her, making her believe that we would not have loved her if we'd known the truth. Yet she still had it in her heart to love us all unconditionally.

Whatever trauma we suffer, we will suffer over and over if it is not faced. Mum should have been told it was not her fault; she needed to forgive herself. It's what I have had to learn too. I have made so many mistakes and have known the very worst of human behaviour but I won't let it define who I am or what I do any more. I have known goodness, too – the patience of friends and family – and that is what I now try to stay true to.

I think about Dad a good deal. I cannot forgive what he did yet I also accept that I grew to love him, and that I was glad to have had the chance to rebuild our relationship and to allow him to be part of my life.

And I think about Mum every day. I mourn her each day

and think of all the things that we will not be able to share, hearing her laugh and wondering what she would have made of my life now. But she gives me joy and hope too, hope that I will be able to honour her memory and hope that one day, perhaps, I will be able to find someone and have a family of my own. And in that way her legacy, as a grandmother, will live on, as one of unconditional love.

AFTERWORD:
2013

Does time heal? I'm not sure. I don't pretend to have answers for everyone but in the six years that have passed since I finished this book, I have learned some things.

Grief is not a journey where the steps are set and certain. Since losing both parents, I have met others whose lives have been marred by tragedy and some are still lost to trauma and pain. How do you regain the life you once had? It isn't possible when you are left without those you love but I hope that it is possible to find a new way to live.

People who meet me are sometimes surprised by how much I laugh and how much I seem to enjoy the day to day, imagining that I don't look back on all that happened. But that isn't true. Each February I think of Mum as her birthday approaches and, as each year passes, I'm aware of how close I am to the age that she was when she was killed. I realise afresh the enormity of all that was denied to her.

It is not just anniversaries. At other times, I'll think of a funny thing that I would like to have told her, or I'll sit down at the end of a shift and watch something on TV that I know she would have enjoyed. It is at these times that I feel a mix of loss but some comfort too as I think of her, the smiling and laughing mum who lit up when she saw her youngest son Daniel. To me, she can never be just the woman who had to endure my father's bullying and control.

We are each of us more than one person, we mean different things to different people and hold within us many contradictions and possibilities. Yet as time passed, I felt I was losing a sense of the kind, thoughtful and loving mother who lived within me. To the outside world, she was 'a victim'. When her name cropped up on the internet, it was as victim. When people met me and came to know my story, Mum was the murder victim, and I the daughter of a killer. Realising that, perhaps I should have accepted that it isn't odd that some people are surprised that I can enjoy my life. After all, what was Elva Aggiano's legacy but one of murder and tragedy? What was I but an orphan to death and betrayal?

I still work at the airport; I still have my colleagues, siblings and my closest friends who help make my life one that I take pleasure in. But as time moved on, the legacy of what my mum's death had become was becoming harder to bear. It was a feeling that I couldn't seem to push aside for long, this sense that my real mother would be lost forever to the grim summary of her last few hours. She was more, so much more, and deserved more.

I didn't know how to change that or even if it would be possible and yet it stayed with me, along with the hope that one day, the sum of Mum's life would add up to more than her death. When the idea came, I don't think I realised that it would lead to something momentous or that it would transform the life of someone I had not met, but it can be the case that, by following the smallest thread, we move into a wholly different world.

Someone I worked with had kidney problems. I knew of the hardship it could bring as kidney illnesses can be debilitating. We talked about organ donation and I learnt that it is possible to donate a kidney even if you are not a family member or a genetic match. At the back of my mind, I thought: 'Mum would have loved to have known that'. She had always been fascinated by medical advances and had wanted to be a nurse. She had even returned to college, before my dad forced her to quit. Before she gave up, I remember how much she had enjoyed the return to learning and how animated she would become when explaining how the body worked and how medical intervention could save lives. We would watch reality programmes together about hospitals and mum would be transfixed when a major operation was filmed. I found the sight alarming until she explained what was happening and then I would be as glued to watching the skilled surgeons and their teams as she was.

I was about 11 years old when Mum told me about organ donor cards. She carried one and despite the fact that I was squeamish about what would happen if my eyes were donated, I still wanted to carry one too. Eventually, Mum agreed and I was very proud to think that if I was to die in a road traffic accident, my organs might be able to save others. After all, they would be no use to me.

Many years later, I watched the film *Pay It Forward*, where the characters are encouraged to repay one good deed by carrying out three good deeds for others. The hope is that as the acts of kindness spread, the world will become a better place. From what I could remember, one of the good deeds should be something significant, something that the recipient could not achieve on their own. I thought that doing three good things was a positive thing to do and I decided I wanted to do one big thing and two smaller ones.

Somehow, these ideas and memories started to merge and in 2010, I decided to research kidney donation. After reading about the stories of those who had decided to donate and the difference it made to the lives of those who received kidneys, I felt a strong sense that not only was it right for me but that my mum would have made the decision right alongside me. Here was my chance to honour Mum and to move on from her memory being dark and terrible to being full of hope.

A few days later, the information pack arrived and I became convinced that it was something I wanted to pursue, but I knew that even if I had made the decision in my head, there was a long way to go. The process was incredibly thorough. There are a number of medical tests that involve blood and urine tests, x-rays, a full body scan, a stress test to ensure that lung and heart function is as it should be and so on. The blood tests were a challenge as I have a fear of needles but every time I was called on to have blood taken, I just took a deep breath, gabbled nervously and hoped for the best. I can't imagine what the nurses made of this woman who was happy to consider giving away a kidney when giving a tiny blood sample caused her to have the wobbles.

Even though all the tests revealed that I was a suitable candidate, you need to be more than fit and healthy to donate; the reasons *why* you have made the decision are tested too. It makes sense of course as to many people risking your life by enduring a major operation, living without a vital organ when you may have need of it at some future point and doing so to help someone you have not met sounds insane. I spoke with my closest friend Jo and, as ever, she listened and said simply that she would support me. Her support would prove invaluable, although I had no idea just how much at this point.

My sister Daiana and brother Daniel viewed things differently. Daiana was very concerned about the risks involved and I could sense that she was opposed to the whole idea. Daniel was more supportive but asked that I record a message for him in case I did not survive the operation. He didn't want to forget my voice; something we both felt we'd lost when thinking about Mum. Perhaps this wasn't fair of me, acting in a way that made my brother and sister feel vulnerable once more, and so it was only right that I was questioned about my motivation.

'Tell me about your parents,' was the psychologist's opening question. He'd been assigned to review my suitability and I thought, 'I wonder how long you've got?'

His concern was that I might be acting out of 'survivor's guilt'. It is not surprising that he'd want to explore that; did I feel guilty that I had survived, the girl who had so often been the target of dad's wrath, whilst my kind-hearted mother had not? I turned his questions over in my mind during the session and for a long time afterwards too.

I tested myself as I needed to know that the positive attitude I was approaching the donation with was genuine and not coming from some sense of misplaced remorse. The idea didn't ring true for me. In the past, when I had hidden how I felt from myself, when I had been foolish or selfish or thoughtless, I could sense in my gut that I was out of kilter and lying to myself. This wasn't how I felt now. Now I felt wholly positive, optimistic about the life-changing opportunity donation can offer someone else and I had a strong yet simple conviction that mum would understand. I even believe that she would have donated before me and that took me back to the awful night of her death.

I had remembered that she carried a donor card. I remember asking if her organs had been used. They hadn't, but why? Was it the post-mortem; was it not possible for a murder victim to donate? Had she been dead for too long for her organs to be viable? I didn't know then and I still don't know now but I remember thinking how sad that would have made Mum. It sounds odd, that in the midst of such overwhelming horror and tragedy such a detail came to me, but shock and grief follow no logic. It felt only right that all these years later, I would be able to do something that Mum would have been proud to support.

After talking through my decision once again with a

panel, there to ensure that I was in no doubt of the risks involved in a major operation and to reassure me that at any point, I could withdraw my consent, I was approved to act as a donor. There was one surprise waiting for me. My tissue was analysed to see which ethnic group my kidney would prove the best match for. Despite being half-Italian, the tests revealed that I would be unsuitable for a recipient whose genetic type matched that found commonly in southern Europe. My as yet unknown recipient would have northern European heritage, or more specifically the genetic characteristics typically found in Scotland or Ireland. That struck me as extraordinary as my mum's family had Scottish roots. She seemed to be part of me as never before.

I did not expect the call so quickly. It came two days after I had officially joined the donation register. Rather than panic, I called Jo, who had been instrumental in my becoming a donor. I would not have been accepted unless someone had stepped forward to say that they would care for me for six weeks after the operation, and she hadn't hesitated. I spoke to my family and informed work. They had been more helpful than I expected and informed me that I would be allowed leave for up to six months. Then all that was left to do was pack and prepare myself for what lay ahead. I didn't feel scared, I felt eager to carry through on the decision I had made.

Perhaps I hadn't really taken in the discomfort that would be involved; perhaps it isn't even possible if you have not been through a major procedure to imagine what post-operative recovery will be like. Ignorance was on my side somewhat as I made my way to the hospital. I wanted to go on my own. I didn't want friends or family going through any more than they had to. Some time before, I had recorded my message for Daniel and that was bad enough. I could not hold the tears back as of course I knew that if Daniel ever watched and listened to it, it would be because I hadn't made it through the procedure. But the tears weren't for me. I wouldn't know anything about it and I had accepted the risks with open eyes. I just didn't want to think of Daniel enduring more loss.

So why was I putting him at risk? This tick-tock played out in my mind but I had to be rational and focus on the fact that although there was risk, it was not substantial. The surgical team were highly experienced and I had to put my trust in them.

Arriving at the hospital, I was calm and soon began to hear stories of others in the Kidney Unit receiving treatment. There were two men who were taken aback by what I was doing. They had debilitating illnesses and it reaffirmed what my operation would mean for whoever would receive my kidney. And who was it? I had only basic details and that was all I wanted to know. He was male, in his forties, had an acute illness, lived within a two-hour drive of the hospital and, critically, had no relative with a match close enough to donate. How odd, I thought; here was a total stranger that I was a perfect match for.

I was calm in the lead-up to the operation – although, as ever, worried about needles – and I made a request of the surgical team that some might think bizarre. I asked them to take a photograph of my kidney. It might sound odd but again, I thought that it would be the kind of thing that Mum would understand and be intrigued by too.

The operation ran entirely to plan. Once I came round from the anaesthetic, my first thought was not about what has happened but about how I would control the pain and discomfort I felt. There was a scar on my left side, below my rib, but the pain wasn't so much as a result of the removal of my kidney, it was more to do with muscle bruising as the lower abdomen is cut into to reach the kidney. I was in intensive care for 24 hours and then moved to a general ward. The next few days were difficult and truthfully, when my pain was being managed correctly, I didn't give the recipient of my kidney a thought. I just wanted to start feeling well again.

A nurse did inform me that the man who had received my kidney was doing really well. It was good to know but the only other highlight of my day was being given ice cubes to relieve my thirst. My focus became being able to leave the hospital as I just didn't feel that I would turn the corner to recovery until I was at Jo's home and fully rested.

Jo and her family were fantastic, I truly could not have asked for more. The ups and downs of my life have taught me that you can enjoy friendships but you find out very little about someone when things go well; it is when life takes a turn for the worst that people's true colours emerge. Being taken into Jo's family and being cared for over what would amount to three months is a debt I'm not sure I can ever repay. After two weeks, I felt well enough to be back on my feet but Jo wasn't convinced. Sure enough, I was silly enough to attempt to lift some heavy shopping and managed to give myself a hernia which put me back a bit, but by week four I felt that life would soon be back to normal.

Twelve weeks is a long time to host a house guest but Jo took it in her stride. I wanted to return to work and felt that three months was a good time to get back to my routine. The job I do isn't desk bound, it is physical and so I think if I'd tried to return before that, I'd just have slowed my team down. Although I was looking forward to seeing all my workmates, going back to live on my own was making me feel nervous. I'd become accustomed to a busy house where I could hear Jo's children playing and laughing and I guessed that the silence once I shut the door of my flat would be oppressive at first.

At work, people asked if I wasn't curious to know about who was walking around with my old kidney. I wasn't, as that would defeat the purpose of making an anonymous donation. There have been difficulties in other countries after donations when donors and recipients have met; apparently a few donors have made direct or indirect requests for money, perhaps suggesting that the recipient and their family 'owed' them. It may be a rare occurrence but I could understand completely why meetings are discouraged.

What is allowed, and seen as positive, is an exchange of letters, via the transplant coordinator. As I sat down to write my letter, I realised that it would be brief. I simply wanted to say that I was pleased to have been in a position to help someone and hoped that their life would now be much easier and enjoyable. Reading it over, it seemed such a few words to encompass all that had happened in the last year and it made me smile to think of what a talking point my decision had been to so many people. I was staggered to find people I didn't know give full vent to their argument of why I was being stupid, or ill-informed, or that I would regret it. One woman give me a stiff lecture about how bad I would feel if I had a child who one day needed a kidney transplant. I asked if she would give up one of her own kidneys if her child needed it. 'Of course,' she said, so I asked her what she would do if it turned out she wasn't a tissue match for her child. 'Then', I said, 'you'll have to rely on people like me and lots of others that I hope will also donate.' All in all, there had been a great deal more many words expended than the few that I now put down on the page for my old kidney's new owner.

Soon afterwards, a letter came via the coordinator and I knew who it was from. What I hadn't expected was two letters. The first was from the recipient, a man called Chris who thanked me for changing his life. Within two days of the operation, he had felt better than he had done in years and within a week he was driving. Soon afterwards had returned to work and now he was planning to marry. It was great to read and I felt that it was all that I had hoped for. But it was the second letter that moved me to tears. It was from Chris's mother and unlike the brief pages that Chris and I had exchanged, this letter ran to over four pages as she recounted what it had been like to see her son's life almost destroyed.

Legionnaires' disease contracted four years earlier had damaged Chris's kidneys irreparably. It was a struggle for him to continue to work as three days a week he had to leave at 4pm for dialysis and would not get home until 10.30pm. He was exhausted and when it become clear that she, her husband and her other son were unable to donate, hope seemed to fade.

Chris's family, like many families, only found that they have irregularities with their kidneys or heart function once they are screened. They were then eliminated as donors and the chances of their relative receiving a healthy kidney diminished. By 2010, Chris's mother had feared that the Christmas they spent together could be their last. That someone would risk their lives to donate to a stranger seemed incredible to her and she was grateful beyond measure. Reading the letter, reading about her anguish and then her joy, made me think that this could have been my mother. Parts of the letter were heartbreaking and I wanted to give her the biggest hug. I think it was only at that moment that I felt the enormity of all that had happened and I felt overwhelmed that the outcome had transformed not only Chris's life but all who knew and loved him. And no one can love quite like a mother. Both letters had moved me and I wrote back but I heard nothing further.

For me, life went on and my body continued to function as normal. I noticed that my scar tingles when it gets very cold; I don't mind, it's quite comforting to be reminded that there is a unique story behind it. Although it is not that unique as I was told that I was the 53rd person in the UK to become an 'altruistic donor'. I hope the number rises.

The *Daily Mirror* found out about my story in 2012 and I spoke to their reporter about my hopes that my mother's story would now be remembered a little differently. What I hadn't expected was for people to remember my story and later that year, I received a call to say that I had been nominated for a Pride of Britain Award. I didn't believe it at first and had to call the journalist back just to check. By this point, I had found out more about my recipient, Chris, through the charity Give A Kidney. His story matched the circumstances of my donation but he said that although he and his mother had written a letter to me, they had heard nothing in return. I realised that my reply must have gone missing and this bothered me. As Chris's surname was an unusual one, I typed it in online and an accountancy firm came up. I sent an email saying, 'I think you may have my kidney'. It was the start of a long correspondence and eventually, we agreed to meet up for Sunday lunch. It was a very special day; Chris and his family are truly lovely and I could not be happier to have met them. We may meet up once a year or so as it is a pretty extraordinary connection but beyond that, I think I should maintain a certain distance. At no point would I want them to feel beholden to me in any way.

The Pride of Britain Awards were held in October 2012 and I was told that the panel of judges included Aled Jones, Emma Bunton and Carol Vorderman. I would be invited to the awards night and a dinner the evening before, with the panel and other nominees, and I would be allowed to bring along Jo and Daniel. It all seemed surreal and I thought I'd receive another call to say there had been a mistake or that I wouldn't be needed after all. The night before, we were to stay in a hotel in central London and the dinner went well;

people were very friendly and that helped calm my nerves. But on the night itself, I felt my confidence drain away. The room was amazing and there were so many familiar faces around, from Olympic diver Tom Daley to comedian John Bishop to entertainer Jason Donavan. In fact, every time I turned my head there was someone I recognised and then it would dawn on me it was because they were famous. It was pretty disorientating and I'd been told that I would be required to go up on stage during the awards. The prospect started to make me feel queasy. In fact, I felt so ill that I could not eat any of the three-course meal provided and I kept asking Jo if I could go home.

If I could have pressed a button and magically have been whisked away to my flat, I would have pressed it. The stories I heard from the award winners were truly humbling and it was hard not to be moved to tears or be awestruck by people's courage. When the signal came that I was next, I felt light-headed but Jo was steadying me as ever. Jon Bon Jovi handed me my award; it was extraordinary, as was the after-awards activity where photographers took what felt like a million pictures. I don't think I'd like to live on the red carpet. People call out your name and it is impossible to know what to do or where to look. What I did like was that Jon Bon Jovi knew how to pronounce my name. Photographers were calling out 'Natalia!' as you might hear the name if it were Russian, the emphasis on the second 'a' of my name. Perhaps because he has Italian heritage, Jon said, 'No, it's Natalia,' with the middle of my name sounding like 'tal' – perfect.

Perhaps the most poignant moment was meeting a lady

in the ladies' room and we chatted for a while about the difficulties of living with a kidney illness. Dialysis can take eight hours a day and is gruelling when there is no prospect of recovery in sight. The lady's daughter then joined us and we talked some more; it took a few minutes for me to realise that the younger woman was Alexandra Burke and it was clear that she was desperately worried about her mother's health. It drove home again that no matter who you are, illness can blight every family and it can cause years of struggle and anguish.

So many people were truly lovely. Louis Walsh for example was very sweet, as was Peter Andre who asked if I would sign a copy of my book for him. It was an odd moment; I was signing a book, not him, and I was amazed when his girlfriend Emily told me that she had already read it and had enjoyed it. Somehow, the whole evening felt unreal and I was glad to be able to get back to the hotel and replay all that had happened and try to remind myself what it had really all been about. There are about seven thousand people waiting for a kidney transplant, including over a hundred children, and many die before they receive an organ. Around three thousand transplants take place each year but there are simply far too few kidneys donated to keep pace with need.

Medical breakthroughs may yet find a way to make transplants unnecessary but that breakthrough is likely to be years away. However, I'm very hopeful that as more people learn about altruistic donations, more people will consider it and decide that it is a step they can take.

It still strikes me as extraordinary that I was part of Pride of Britain. It was very humbling and I still feel honoured to have been considered, let alone to have won. But how did I become part of the awards in the first place? It puzzled me as I had not put myself forward and I had not seen any publicity advertising who people could vote for. It seemed odd. Then I was told that when the votes came in, few people could remember my name as it is a bit of a mouthful. They had voted for 'the girl who donated a kidney to honour her mum'.

That was it. It was all I could have hoped for. My mum's story has changed; she is now remembered for something that benefitted one man in the most remarkable way, brought relief and joy to his family and may even prompt others to act altruistically. I know that she would have been delighted and it is how I'd like us both to be remembered. I think of her every day and feel certain that she knows that her little girl is doing just fine. What more can I ask for?

In memory of Simon Waller